THE SUBMERGED FEMININE:
THE SYMBOL OF THE MERMAID IN THE HUMAN PSYCHE

by
Gillian Pothier

Submitted in partial fulfillment of the requirements
for the degree of

MASTER OF ARTS IN COUNSELING PSYCHOLOGY

Pacifica Graduate Institute
15 March 2011

I certify that I have read this paper and that in my opinion it conforms to acceptable standards of scholarly presentation and is fully adequate, in scope and quality, as a product for the degree of Master of Arts in Counseling Psychology.

Thomas Elsner, J.D., M.A.
Faculty Advisor

On behalf of the thesis committee, I accept this paper as partial fulfillment of the requirements for Master of Arts in Counseling Psychology.

Thomas Elsner, J.D., M.A.
Research Coordinator

On behalf of the Counseling Psychology program, I accept this paper as partial fulfillment of the requirements for Master of Arts in Counseling Psychology.

Wendy Davee, M.A., M.F.T.
Chair, Counseling Psychology Program

Abstract

THE SUBMERGED FEMININE:
THE SYMBOL OF THE MERMAID IN THE HUMAN PSYCHE

by Gillian Pothier

This thesis explores the symbol of the mermaid within the human psyche and its corollary relationship to the submerged feminine principle. The framework for exploring this image is multifaceted and draws upon mythology, poetry, fairy tale, art, and dream imagery.

The research methodology used within this thesis is dual-pronged: the *raison d'être* for this subject was breathed into life via the principle of an alchemical hermeneutical orientation, and a hermeneutic wing allowed for a more consciously participatory engagement with the archetypal dimensions of this image. The 19th century French fairy tale entitled *Undine* and the 19th century Danish fairy tale entitled *The Little Mermaid* are used as auxiliary lenses with which to explore the symbol of the mermaid within a narrative scaffolding. Certain psychic realities can only be expressed by a symbol, and the living image of the mermaid is indeed charged with potent symbolic and archetypal meaning.

Acknowledgements

My heart wanders back to all those who have lifted me up along the way…
I count my lucky stars for each of you.

To Jeremy, speaker of the truth…for opening heart and home,
and for putting ketchup on his ketchup.

To Jennifer and Jessica…for grounding my life in deep and authentic friendship, and for being sparkly beacons of encouragement and faith at every crossroad along the way.
I am such a lucky girl.

To Tom Elsner…for holding steady,
and inviting me to fall in love with fairy tales all over again.

To my editrix extraordinaire, Liza Gerberding…for her *multifold* and *synechdochic* talents, and for making me giggle when otherwise I may have cried.
I am so grateful.

To little Roxie…for sneaking in when I wasn't looking, for warming toes and heart,
and for making me laugh every day.

To the professors and staff of Pacifica…for sharing your laughter and brilliance.

And to my rabble-rousing sweet cohort…
big lizard love…may the long-time sun shine upon you.

To the memory of my father, Ritchie, whose blood I feel coursing within my own each day.

And to the mermaids.

Dedication

To my mother, Elizabeth,
for whispering in the ear of her little girl that
"everything will be ok,"
and even when it wasn't,
it always was.
You are my north star.

Table of Contents

Chapter I
Introduction

Overview

The long way to you is still tied to me – but it
brought me to you
I keep wanting to give you what is already yours

W. S. Merwin, as cited in Downing, 2007, p. 86

My journey with the mermaids is one that has only begun fairly recently. I did not grow up as a little girl with a coterie of mermaid figures or with any particular penchant towards this image. I lived in New York City for 12 years during my 20s and early 30s, famous for its annual Mermaid Parade held within the streets of Coney Island, and did not attend its celebration once. And yet, during my two years at Pacifica, I slowly fell under the spell of the symbol of the mermaid and observed curiously as she wound her way into and through multiple papers that I wrote, even when her presence felt remote and perhaps not even topically salient. I was curious about her slow but persistent appearance within my academic world, and found myself increasingly willing to open myself to whatever it may be that she longed to reveal, recalling the formidable question posed by Meri Lao, celebrated Fellini composer and Italian author of a quintessential book about the lore of the mermaid: "How many women could have identified with these lost goddesses, bearers of a message to which man is afraid to listen?" (1998/2007, p. 100). Even as I began to conceptually engage the idea of writing a thesis, the idea of writing about the symbol of the mermaid was secondary to an idea that at the time felt much more “interesting” to me. However, insistently and silently, the living symbol of the mermaid came alive for me, holding me in her mythological embrace by day, and lurking so viscerally in my dreams at night that I would wake with my legs aching from being so tightly bound by the constraints of an imaginal fish’s tail the night before. In an inverted polarity that remains startling to me, it was my human legs that ached from being so tightly bound in my dreams, just as it was with Hans Christian Andersen’s Little Mermaid, whose newly bifurcated human legs caused her to feel as though “she were treading on sharp knives or pricking gimlets” (Andersen, 1837/1976, p. 57) with each step of her new human consciousness. I became increasingly present to the pain of meeting the mermaid aspect of my self, of opening my self to her grief, her song of sorrow and longing. I was also becoming progressively aware of the pain inherent within the journey of writing this thesis, newly conscious to the reality that each step forward was harkened with pain, just as the Little Mermaid’s “graceful walk” was fluent to the world around her, but vestiges of “sharp knives” was her private corpulent experience. (The metaphor of waking from a dream in pain carries deep meaning: most overtly perhaps the reverie of a first lost love.) As the moon gave way to the light of day and I awoke to reality of morning, my body ached, my legs alive with re-membering the fish’s tail that, like a phantom limb, lived just below my pedestrian consciousness. I knew that the mermaids were calling me to witness them, to listen to their story, to remember. Ultimately, I bowed to their beckoning and now recognize the honor of being called to witness “her,” to remember the mermaids that have swum beside us, and too, those that walk amongst us.

Researching mermaid imagery and symbolism leads one on a nutritive and diverse pilgrimage to the mythological singing sirens of ancient Greece, and no less, to the aisles of a present-day toy store, where glittering and unctuous Mermaid Barbies silently beckon from beyond their paralyzed smiles. With their reductive and sanitized commercialization, these bite-sized iconoclastic plastic dolls simultaneously depotentiate and make diminutive two feminine archetypes: the goddess and the mermaid. As an anachronistic and more formal counterpoint to the modern embodiment of the mermaid, one begins to find stories of mortals who were dangerously seduced by the songs of the spirits associated with the sea as early as Homer's *Odyssey* (c. 8th century BCE).

There are, quite literally, hundreds of goddesses hailing from across cultures associated with the water and with the moon, the celestial counterpoint to the watery feminine depths. Aphrodite, the goddess of love and beauty, is famously known for being born from the sea and is recognized as the goddess associated with feminine wholeness: "She is present when wholeness emerges from the halves and when the resolved opposites become the indissolvable goldeness of life" (Kerenyi, as cited in Downing, 2007, p. 202). Throughout history and mythology, one sees an intermingling of the feminine with water and with the moon, as well as mermaids with goddess imagery and iconography. Even today, we see the alchemical icon of a two-tailed mermaid etched into the seemingly omnipresent Starbucks logo. It is said the "two tails represent unity—of earth and water, body and soul . . . the all-pervading *anima mundi" ("Melusine," 2010, para. 3)*. The archetype of the mermaid remains extraordinarily widespread amongst cultures, crossing language, time, and artistic barriers, which perhaps speaks vividly to its ancient ability to fulfill a specific need in the human collective unconsciousness. Within the more empirical light of present day, it is commonly thought that the moon affects both the tide as well as women's menstrual cycles, again corroborating the feminine mystique associated with water and lunar activity.

Elements of mermaid mythology, and specifically, the tale of de la Motte Fouque's (1814/2002) *Undine*, have woven themselves into various artistic initiatives, pointing to the quixotic and possibly archaic unconscious appeal of these divine sea enchantresses. Literature, too, reflects the embodiment of the enchanting spell of the mermaid. One such example, a poem I have loved my entire adulthood, is T. S. Eliot's singular modern poetic triumph, "*The Love Song of J. Alfred Prufrock" (1917),* of which the last glorious stanza I will include here:

> I have heard the mermaid singing, each to each.
> I do not think they will sing to me.
>
> I have seen them riding seaward in the waves
> Combing the white hair of the waves blown back
> When the wind blows the water white and black.
>
> We have lingered in the chambers of the sea
> By sea-girls wreathed with seaweed red and brown
> Till human voices wake us, and we drown. (2001, p. 7)

In both music and painting, the legend of water nymphs has long ago cast its illusory spell. I personally recall one of my earliest seductions into the world of mermaid mythology when viewing Sir John Everett Millais' hauntingly lovely painting, *Ophelia* (1852). While not specifically of the mermaid canon, there was something immediately evocative about this painting to me. I felt like I had long imagined such an immersion or descent into the regressive innocence of water in its natural, instinctual form, but that this longing somehow lived below consciousness. In ways that remain distinctly feminine but ineffable to me, when viewing this painting, it felt more like a remembrance—a recognition of an archaic knowing—than a visual encounter. I could almost *feel* the way Ophelia may have felt, singing just moments prior to her watery death, and indeed, did not know she was dead in her descent down the river until I later read more about the painting and of course, became more intimate with Shakespeare's *Hamlet*, from which the character of Ophelia emerged. I was in my early 20s at this time, and felt richly and newly stirred by the poignancy of this experience. It was the beginning, perhaps, of my archetypal engagement with this particular chthonic feminine aspect. To continue with the contemporary contextualization of the mythos and symbology of the mermaid, a slightly more pop-cultural example of this collective fascination with the feminine and water is a rather (in)famous bar in New York City, where I lived for a long time prior to moving to Los Angeles. It was called the Coral Bar, and was nestled in the at the time still bourgeoning neighborhood of Chelsea. In this highly stylized and chic bar, there were surrounding large, wall-sized water tanks and young men and women would dress the part of mermaid/merman, complete with shimmering sequined tales, and slip into the rather erotically backlit velvety waters. I found myself riveted once again by confronting the feminine immersion into the dark waters, despite the full awareness of performance and fictional embellishment. Despite an entire lack of nudity, there was a profound nakedness and sensuality in the experience of watching, of witnessing. It felt somehow voyeuristic, latently erotically charged: an aquatic and costumed peepshow. It was not only I, however, who found the watery descent somehow mesmerizing; the lounge was often filled to capacity with chic Manhattan-ites, Cosmos in hand and eyes transfixed on the sinewy water nymphs. I was sad to see that the Coral Bar has subsequently closed as it seemed to fulfill, at least for me, an encounter once again with this sensual fascination with the feminine and its relationship to water.

Clearly, some aspect of my psyche is bewitched by the imago of the mermaid. As a child, I was all but utterly disinterested in this bizarre hybrid creature, but as I unfolded, and continue to unfold as a woman, I increasingly hear the exquisitely seductive song of this sea-chanteuse. The ability—and difficulty—of having to learn to live in two uniquely different worlds is something that I intimately recognize. This is not due to a geographical or even physical circumstance, but is altogether psychic: I often feel outside of our popular culture, as though part of me lives somewhere else, one foot on land, one foot in the Other world—the world of water.

> The Other world is a pulsing, inspired realm right next to the world of measurements and facts. . . . It is the inner-world and underworld, ever alive with birds that speak and shining cities under the waves. The Other world remains in the depths of memory just as certainly as the ancient paintings that waited to be discovered in prehistoric caves. (Meade, 2006, p. 89)

One aspect of the figure of the mermaid longs for consciousness, for individuation, for expression and voice; this is her upper torso, the part of her that is personal, specific, and reflective of an ego-state, a persona. However, the lower region of the mermaid remains hidden under the surface, is submerged, collective, and instinctive. I recognize this duality as something that is true for me: the longing to remain hidden and "beneath the surface" *and* the longing to have voice, to be fully expressed in the outer world. In some ways, perhaps this duality is akin to C. G. Jung's personality No. 1 and No. 2 (Jung, 1961/1989, p. 45).

Additionally—and more personally—there is something deeply poignant and symbolic about the need for a mermaid (and Undine, specifically) to marry a mortal man in order to be ensouled. As I am not yet married, I was surprisingly and rather painfully struck by how deeply this resonated for me. Of course, I have a soul—but there is part of my psyche that feels as though it is straining to awaken, and knows that it may only do so within the alchemical retort of sacred union. "Relationships offer containers for the craziness. The deeper they go, the more they can hold. They provide places for sacrifice and for protection against the destructive aspect of the creative" (Hillman, 1972, p. 38). It remains fascinating to me how an image once deflated of meaning or interest can slowly place the individual psyche within its gaping but benevolent mouth, or silently bat us about with its mythic paw. "The invisible energy of the psyche scavenges the known and unknown for images to become hosts for meaning. Such image-husks are filled with energy and present themselves dynamically for the possibility of conscious discernment" (Hollis, 2000, p. 18). It is so with my mermaids. They are living symbols: teacher, mother, lover, divine child, and sister alike, and have taught me that soul-making entails soul-destroying—the perfect metaphor for entering into the creative matrix of analysis and relationship alike.

Guiding Purpose

I am led by both overt and subtle guiding principles in the unfolding of this thesis. On a metaphorical and perhaps metaphysical realm, I am aware that honoring the archetypal symbol of the mermaid is an aspect of my vocational calling. "The original meaning of 'to have a vocation' is 'to be addressed by a voice'" (Jung, 1954/1977, p. 176). In a sense, it is clear to me that I have been "addressed by a voice," although in the instance of the mermaid, it is perhaps more suitable to refer to the process of being called to listen to her haunting song. Second, and in light of a more clinical counterpoint, I am profoundly clear about the relationship between the symbol of the mermaid and the loss of the chthonic feminine within modern American culture. The symbol of the mermaid is very much alive, although increasingly depotentiated, within our animus-possessed culture. As inhabitants of a highly industrialized culture, we struggle to carry our primitive aspect, our physically invisible tail, dragging it along behind us. To encounter the tail, that aspect of self we can perhaps no longer see, is to integrate shadow contents that remain very much psychically alive.

Rationale

The symbol of the mermaid provides an ancient gossamer thread of connectivity between multiple psychological and cultural aspects, perhaps most notably and metaphorically speaking to the lost feminine aspect within self and culture. The resurrection and reclamation of this symbol archetypally is a central tenet of this thesis, and one which I believe holds a healing function intrapsychically. The mermaid may initially present as a segregated and bifurcated form, but slowly reveals "herself" to be a symbol pointing towards psychic wholeness. This recognition requires an immersion into the watery realms of the mythopoeic, the archetypal imagination, and the feminine. In many ways, the journey towards the archetypal significance of the mermaid (and likely towards all archetypal imagery) is precisely the same "descent" that the analytic encounter both requires and cultivates. It is my belief that the exploration of the intrapsychic relationship to an archetypal experience is deeply congruent with the interpsychic relationship that occurs within the *temenos* of the therapeutic container. The exploration of the relationship to symbol and to archetype—particularly one that invokes a descent towards the feminine—feels very much alive with psychological relevance (if not revelation) within the canon of counseling psychology.

Research Methodology

> I do not ever truly have ideas; they have, hold, contain, govern me. Our wrestling with ideas is a sacred struggle, as with an angel.
>
> Hillman, 1975, p. 130

The primordial and universal wisdom inherent within mythology and fairy tale is a theoretical polestar within this archetypal exploration of the symbol of the mermaid. Myth simultaneously encapsulates and reveals—often drawing potent synechdochic qualities of illumination or revelation from symbol or metaphor. This language of myth—both as embodied narrative as well as the significance of story *in and of itself*—remains both fundamentally encoded within the landscape of fairy tale and psyche alike, yet inextricably calls forth to be known, to be named. With the intention of widening my understanding of myth and fairy tale, specifically regarding the living symbol of the mermaid, I will more deeply and consciously turn towards the seminal landscape of art, poetry, cosmogonic symbology, and the alchemical and archetypal underpinnings of fairy tale. In doing so, I further hope to draw towards mc an appropriate and fertile methodology of inquiry. One that, like Nature itself, allows for and seeks relationship between opposites and reveals not only an early primary imago of conceptualization, but one that remains spacious and supple, allowing for cultivation, discernment, and growth. I hope to imbue rather than impose and find opportunities to risk of myself, to share the intermittently lost little mermaid I carry within, and the passionate and noble surrender of Undine that at times I so greatly fear.

Despite the overarching analytic character of this inquiry, I do not want this process to be a purely teleological and intellectual pursuit. I want to be courageous enough to allow illumination to emerge from the interstices, to give voice to the gnostic sensuality of my own body, to bring forth the nutritive soils of my own life—its unique raptures, its scarlet sorrows, and its darkly omniscient shadows.

The framework for approaching a methodology of research within this thesis is essentially that of an alchemical hermeneutical orientation. Depth psychologist and author Robert Romanyshyn identified an experience of being called by the topic through one's own unconscious psychical complexes as opposed to consciously selecting one's subject:

> Perhaps the path or method of research done with soul in mind is simply a recognition that all our acts of knowing are attempts at remembering what we once knew but have forgotten. Perhaps all our attempts at re-search are sacred acts whose deep motive is salvation or redemption. (2007, p. 268)

Within this orientation exists the rather delicate assumption of an autonomous and dynamic collective unconscious. Depth psychology teaches us that the unconscious surrounds us; it infuses the world with the mystery of the ineffable and an unknowable and autonomous dynamism. This pre-supposition is congruent with my constellation of clinical underpinnings, but nonetheless feels important to elucidate.

The secondary mode of researching is that of a hermeneutical nature. A hermeneutical approach is eponymously named in honor of the God of communication, Hermes. "Hermes is the messenger of the gods/goddesses, the link that bridges the human world and the divine, and what Hermes brings to us is the capacity for the symbol by which we are stretched between these two worlds" (Goodchild & Romanyshyn, 2003, p. 23). A hermeneutical orientation involves an active and participatory engagement with the interpretation of written or imagistic symbolic texts. The aspect of hermeneutics that feels particularly intriguing to me is the latent notion of a co-creational impulse:

mermaids and I engage each other in a process of symbolic—and mutual—transformation. My legs ache from being bound within my dreams, but also from my longing for this lost tail. I look down, both palpably relieved and crushed with despair when I see legs where I have felt . . . feel . . . the sinewy amalgam of tail. I am also increasingly present to the reality that the psychic presence of mermaids within my life form a *living relationship* and that "in relationship we move not only with conscious intention but in concert with deeper, more ancient motions, chthonic motives, primal forces, and telluric patterns" (Hollis, 2000, p. 37). In other words, I am profoundly aware that there are both conscious and intentional attributes to my research process, and with a corollary function, that there are also unconscious forces and "deeper, more ancient, chthonic motives" that are very much alive within this process. Ultimately, it becomes a matter of choosing to trust, to have faith, for it is

> truly better to be enveloped in a matter that darkly feeds itself with hidden fires; better not to know fully where the veins of fascination lead, but to trust that they will slowly give up their heat in recompense for attention paid. (Hyde, 1998, p. 90)

Research Problem

Romanyshyn referred to the "the work" as a way of witnessing the wound (2007, p. 76). This is analogous to archetypal psychologist and scholar James Hillman's concept that the "wound and the eye are one and the same" (1991, p. 149). While these lenses provide a fertile entrance into a mythopoeic advancement of the concepts explored in this thesis, they also very much acknowledge the inherent blindnesses and biases of the researcher in that "the eye of the complex gives the peculiar twist we call *psychological insight*" (p. 149). In other words, inherent in the research "problem" is the fact that I am invariably blinded by my own woundedness, my own complexes and torments; my research is inherently subjective; and that it is through my own consciousness that I become aware of an unconscious shadow in my own thinking and researching methodology (Romanyshyn, 2007). Philosopher Friedrich Nietzsche recognized the self-reflexivity within this sort of journey, stating that every great philosophy so far has been "the personal confession of its author and a kind of involuntary and unconscious memoir" (1886/1966, p. 13).

As the literature review will address more comprehensively, very little has been written about the relationship between the symbol of the mermaid and a depth psychological perspective. Hillman identified that "this concern with depth leads us in practice to pay special attention to *whatever is below*" (1991, p. 157). This has dual meaning in reference to the symbol of the mermaid. Mermaids live below the sea, so there is an immediate recognition of the unconscious relevance of this watery underworld. However, mermaids themselves are duplex creatures—their "below" being comprised of a fish's tail. The recognition of this complexity is not a static process for me, and there are times and moments when I take a deep breath, and gently take flight from the structured scaffolding of a more practical, theoretical approach. Here, I find my way back to theoretical and clinical relevance through poetry, image, and at times, reverie. (I am reminded of a lovely quote by Emerson that very much captures the way I naturally orient to feeling function, to recognizing the "angel aspect" (Hillman, 1975, p. 9) of word or image: "A poem, a sentence, causes us to be ourselves. I be and I see my being, at the same time" (Emerson, 1910, p. 180).

Mermaids are primordial beings, a living metaphor of paradox and fusion between worlds. Half-human and half-fish, they embody the duplex realms of the primitive and the civilized, consciousness and unconsciousness, upper world and underworld, their cleaved nature encapsulating our own ambiguous nature. Mermaids, like their masculine terrestrial counterpart, the minotaur, embody the question surrounding our own conflicted providence: how is it that we as modern human beings can somehow unite the most primitive and acculturated aspects of our selves within our own human existences? From a depth psychological perspective, one can posit the question in terms of exploring ways in which we can hold the tension between the instinctive, erotic, unconscious aspect of the human psyche along with the civilized, refined, and conscious aspect of Self. The term *Self*, as it is being used within the context of this thesis, is a formidable and complex Jungian concept. Notably, within a Jungian theoretical landscape, it is often seen with a capital "S" regardless of its placement within a sentence. Jungian analyst and scholar Marie-Louise von Franz defined *Self* as the "psychic totality of an individual, and also, paradoxically, the regulating center of the collective unconscious. Every individual and every nation has its own modes of experiencing this psychic reality" (1996, p. 2). Jungian analyst June Singer helped to further elucidate this rather complex concept by explaining that "'Self' as Jung used it has a special meaning; it is that center of being which the ego circumambulates; at the same time it is the superordinate factor in a system in which the ego is subordinate" (1994, p. 210).

The reconciliation of the divided within the symbol of the mermaid is a potent metaphor for our own human suffering and distancing from this "center of being which the ego circumambulates" (Singer, 1994, p. 210) and our "own psychic totality" (von Franz, 1996, p. 2) which Jung identified as "Self," and has immediate relevance for the clinician as well as the analysand. An exploration of the symbol of the mermaid within the human psyche will help yield psychic truth and insight about the anima as well as the chthonic forces that live within each of us.

Research Question

How can our most instinctual and primordial impulses be in relationship with the civilized, conscious, and acculturated dimensions of self within our own human existences? How can one hold the tension between the instinctive, erotic, unconscious aspect of the human psyche along with the initiated, refined, and conscious aspect of Self? The reconciliation of these divided impulses and aspects of Self are embodied within the symbol of the mermaid, which becomes a potent metaphor for our own human suffering and distancing from our instinctual and erotic impulses. It is this precise irreconcilable condition of our own chthonic forces implicit within our human experience that has immediate relevance for the clinician. How can we as psychotherapists support our clients in making healthy contact with this archaic and instinctual aspect of self? Is it possible to regulate this encounter within the analytic container?

Synopsis of Chapters

The introduction serves to illuminate my personal and psychological relationship with the symbol of the mermaid. Clinical relevance in the form of research questions begins to guide the orientation of the following chapters. A review of the literature comprises Chapter II, serving to differentiate my own point of view from that which has already been written regarding the archetypal symbol of the mermaid, and how the material written to date either serves to speak to the aforementioned research questions, or how the absence of relevant material thereof also serves to illuminate the interstitial nature of both the symbol of the mermaid and "her" clinical relevance within the field of depth psychology.

Chapter II
Literature Review

> Out of this space, where the anima of the work and I breathe together, the chapter can now begin.
>
> Romanyshyn, 2007, p. 335

This review of the literature that constellates around the living metaphor of the mermaid includes the following lenses: a historical viewpoint (history of mermaids, sirens, and female sea deities), extrapolations within the canon of mermaid literature (*Undine (de la Motte Fouque, 1814/2002), The Little Mermaid (Andersen, 1837/1976), Melusine (14th century)* the feminine within fairy tales (à la von Franz, 1993), and the alchemical attribute of *coincidentia oppositorum* via Eliade (1952/1991) and Jung (1936/1968). While I was able to find rich, scholarly exposition and illumination of the history and cultural implications of the phenomenology of the mermaid, I remained unable to locate a specifically Jungian or depth psychological exploration of this complex symbol. As a result, there has been a deep immersion into the various tomes that explore the mythologem and symbology of the mermaid in order to become facile in my knowledge base of this archetype. The depth psychological link, however, had to be aggregated in a more intimate and personal quest, seeking (and finding) conceptual linkages and relationship to the imaging of the anima, erotic love, the betwixt feminine, and the ineffable but visceral conflict between chthonic feminine primitivity and initiated feminine and cultural consciousness. It becomes important to define what is meant by the word *anima.* Marion Woodman, Jungian analyst and body workshop leader, explained that "in Jungian psychology, we speak of this inner feminine as the *anima*, the Latin word for soul" (1993, p. 146). Woodman expounded upon the relationship between psychology, soul, and anima by stating that "psyche means soul. Psychology is knowledge of the soul. . . . Jung recognized soul. He talked about the soul in a man, *the anima* [emphasis added]" (p. 95).

Singer helped to further draw forth clarity from this Jungian term, and located it within its inherently feminine context:

> Let us begin by trying to understand what Jung meant by the words anima and animus. These he expressed as twin archetypes of the contrasexual: the anima standing for the "eternal feminine" aspect in a man, and the animus representing the "eternal masculine" in a woman. . . . Because of their archetypal connections, anima and animus have been represented in many collective forms and figures: the man's anima may appear as Aphrodite, Marilyn Monroe, Sophia the embodiment of wisdom, or Kali the embodiment of destruction. The possibilities are endless—but these figures are all in some way "bigger than life" and evoke something powerful in us as they appear in dreams or imagination. (1994, p. 179)

While a book dedicated to the depth psychological relevance of the symbol of the mermaid remained elusive, there were, gratefully, many essays, articles, and passages peppering the pages of books written by the great Jungian and post-Jungian authors to shed light upon my inquiry. Marie-Louise von Franz (1993), Ulanov & Ulanov (2004), Monika Wikman (2004), Mircea Eliade (1952/1991), James Hillman (1972, 1975, 1991), and many others illuminated realms of psychological and psychic relevance and relatedness that I had not originally fathomed.

Mermaids in Myth and Fairy Tale

Perhaps the most famous of all mermaid stories is Hans Christian Andersen's (1837/1976) renowned tale of *The Little Mermaid*, published in 1837 in Copenhagen. The fairy tale that originally provided my literary *entrée de passage* towards the archetypal succor of the betwixt feminine, *Undine*, was published in 1814 in Germany (de la Motte Fouque, 1814/2002). *Undine* is a Teutonic novella, and like all mermaid-inspired stories, its ancestry descends from the 14th century French mermaid legend par excellence, *Melusine*. It remains interesting to note that these stories were published within 73 years of each other, all within northern European countries. Notably, both *Undine* and *The Little Mermaid* have found re-embodiment in the medium of film in recent years: *Undine* as a film for adults called *Ondine (Jordan, 2010)*, and *The Little Mermaid* (Musker & Ashman, Clements & Musker, 1989) as Disney's stunningly successful film along with its vast array of Ariel (the name of the mermaid character) product extensions. *Undine* was published 59 years prior to Hans Christian Andersen's *The Little Mermaid*, and many scholars associate de la Motte Fouque's fairy tale noir, *Undine*, which George MacDonald, noted 19th century fantasy scholar, has captured through his declaration "of all fairy tales I know, I think *Undine* the most beautiful" **(2010, para. 2)** as a source of inspiration and influence upon Andersen's story. Given the complexity and ancient ontology of the symbol of the mermaid, it requires a particular literary immersion into its complex ancestry and cultural relevance. However, it is my objective to specifically explore the archetypal, symbolic, and psychic significance of the sea enchantress. To that end, several books and authors have provided vital stepping stones between the symbol of the mermaid and the archetypal world in which she dwells.

Mermaids: A Mythological, Cultural, and Ontological History

As the mermaid is a mythic entity, in many ways, it is not possible to extricate the phenomenology of the mermaid from her historical landscape; her ontology is a reflection of the world in which she is brought forward—may it be through myth, painting, or poem. In light of this, the history of the mermaid intrinsically includes the ways in which she functions as an anima image; the psychic succor of her extraordinary and paradoxical being is contextual *and* archetypal. In my research to date, I have found there to be four contemporary anthologies of the history and trope of the siren/mermaid.

The earliest of these books is folklore and fairy tale book author Peter Lum's 1951 book entitled *Fabulous Beasts*, which is an expansive anthology of the fantastical sentient beings that have historically populated our imaginations. Feminist scholar and author Dorothy Dinnerstein's 1977 feminist classic entitled *Mermaids and Minotaurs: Sexual Arrangements and Malaise (1999)* is considered a seminal and brilliant inquiry into Darwinian principles via a feminist lens, and incorporates an extraordinary understanding of the metaphorical potency of mermaid and minotaur alike. British folklore author Beatrice Phillpotts' eminent anthology of mermaid iconography and meaning, entitled *Mermaids,* appeared in 1980, and focused exclusively on the history and symbology of the mermaid phenomenology.

Perhaps the most significant contribution to my personal immersion into the history and symbolic dynamism of the mermaid was found within *Seduction and the Secret Power of Women: The Lure of Sirens and Mermaids* by the Italian author and Federico Fellini film composer, Meri Lao (1998/2007). This rather lithe book explored the symbology of the mermaid trope historically within the cultural precincts of literature and art, as well as within the human imagination. Lao engaged most directly with the potent symbolic and metaphorical value of the mermaid; she recognized the inherent psychological implications of this feminine mythical figure. Similarly to the other authors, Lao illuminated the historical significance of the symbol of the mermaid and understood the ways in which this symbol is inherently intertwined with the meta perspective of "woman" in each of these particular epochs of time and places within the world. However, Lao amplified this understanding with something that begins to feel like a depth psychological lens. She folded Jungian principles into her inquiry, and provided a rich and diverse array of literary references which further function to reveal the way mermaids and sirens live as timeless imagos of the feminine within the collective unconscious. Lao is an accomplished author and, intriguingly, has composed music for Fellini; she has a lovely, lyrical sensuality to her understanding of the figure of the mermaid. However, she is not a Jungian scholar, so her engagement with Jungian principles such as alchemy or the anima remain touched on, but largely unearthed.

Lao was careful to elucidate that "contrary to what was commonly believed, fish-formed and winged sirens share the same cradle" (1998/2007, p. 100). However, as women become increasingly identified with demonic forces, the serpent's body replaced the Siren's wings (Graham, 2007, p. ix), and from the body of the serpent eventually emerged the tail of the fish that remains potently and synecdochically symbolic of the mermaid. "Thus, we find the first motifs surrounding the symbol of the Sirens: the enchantment, the sacred, instability of form, ambivalence, and transcendental experience" (Lao, 1998/1007, p. 17).

Cross-Cultural Sea Deities and Mermaids

In accordance with Jung's (1948/1969, p. 191 [*CW* 11, para. 285]) understanding of the collective reality of symbols, it is fascinating to recognize that mermaid iconography is found within ancient cultures the world over. Peter Lum's (1951) scholarly inquiry into the omnipotence of the phenomenology of the mermaid and otherworldly creatures is a treasure trove of the fantastical. With scholarly prowess, he is able to readily capture the trans-global presence of mermaid figures and lore:

> The mermaid is found in all Western countries; she is the German Meriminni or Meerfrau, the Icelandic Marmenill, the Danish Maremind, the Irish Merow and many others, and there are echoes of her story from the East, as well. The Matsyanaris, figures sometimes found sculptured in Indian temples, are nymphs with fishes' tails, and superstitious Chinese sailors firmly believe in the existence of similar creatures in the China Sea. (p. 131)

Mermaids are born from the tribe of the in-between, the undecidables: centaurs, minotaurs, satyrs, and cyclops share this indeterminacy and similar fused state of identity. It is their very split nature, this duplicity of identity, that imparts the mermaid and her mythical brothers and sisters with their timeless archetypal potency. Lao, too, spoke to the presence of the "fusion of human and feral aspects" in ancient religions the world over:

> The fusion of human and feral aspects is an emblem venerated in the most ancient religions. Examples include the winged spirits in the Assyrian sculpture in Nimrod, the Babylonian demon Labartu, and the animal-headed stone representations of the Egyptian divinities: Sekmet (lioness), Hathor (cow), Bast (cat), Thoth (ibis), and Horus (falcon). . . . A sizable portion of the beliefs and folklore of the entire planet includes references to human beings transformed into animals and vice versa. (1998/2007, p. 15)

Through these widening anthropomorphic perspectives, it is revealed that mermaids (and other ancient half-human/half-feral creatures) have existed in myth and the human psyche the world over and in many if not all of our earliest civilizations. What is it about such entities that captivates our imagination, that our soul somehow alights to in distant recognition? What is it about this convergence of opposites that mermaids, as bearers of the beyond, give voice to over the millenia and the world across? It remains intriguing and significant from an archetypal perspective that once the symbol of the mermaid incarnated as a half-fish half-woman entity in iconography and literature, there has been very little variance of this convergence of form for thousands of years; this particular dialectic of form encodes erotic duplicity and paradox that remains eloquent and meaningful to the human psyche. "Images, symbols, and myths are not irresponsible creations of the psyche; they respond to a need and fulfill a function, that of bringing to light the most hidden modalities of being" (Eliade, 1952/1991, p. 12). According to renowned professor of religious history and author Mircea Eliade's perspective, the symbol of the mermaid means something both ineffable and "real" to the human psyche; there is a *reason* it exists with such enduring longevity and with relatively little physical historical modification. The symbol of the mermaid is a living psychic product; it is a symbol of our own instinctual wisdom—and perhaps intrinsic torment.

The Lore and Lure of the Mermaid

Dorothy Dinnerstein's (1999) *The Mermaid and the Minotaur* is a remarkable feminist psychoanalytic exploration, often featured in university and graduate social and cultural psychology courses. Dinnerstein provided a fiercely incisive treatise on the psychic and cultural machinations of the feminine, most specifically in its relationship to motherhood, and its intrapsychic implications for both male and female offspring. The book, despite its mythological title, is significantly *not* a book about mermaids nor minotaurs. However, the very fact that Dinnerstein encapsulated much of her socio-anthropological principles within a cursory understanding of the "myth images of half-human beasts" (p. 2) is profoundly evocative. Remarkably, she included only two mentions of mermaids or minotaurs within her entire scholarly exposition, both of which are crystalline examples of the immediacy and potency that these particular imagos generate:

> Myth-images of half-human beasts like the mermaid and the minotaur express an old, fundamental, very slowly clarifying communal insight: that our species' nature is internally inconsistent, that our continuities with, and our differences from, the earth's other animals are mysterious and profound; and in these continuities, and these differences, lie both a sense of strangeness on earth and the possible key to a way of feeling at home here. (p. 2)

In a fascinating but largely subterranean, latent reference to the mermaid's relationship to Eros, Dinnerstein (in her second and final reference to the figure of the mermaid throughout her 295-page book), elucidated the following:

> The images of the mermaid and minotaur have bearing not only on human malaise in general (this they have in common with all creatures of their ilk—harpies and centaurs, werewolves and sphinxes, winged nymphs, goat-eared fauns, and so on—who have fascinated our imaginations) but also on our sexual arrangements in particular. The treacherous mermaid, seductive and impenetrable female representative of the dark and magic underwater world from which our life comes and in which we cannot live, lures voyagers to doom. (p. 5)

While I find Dinnerstein's discourse superbly insightful and cogent, in its entirety, it is not precisely salient or congruent with an exploration of the archetypal relevance of mermaids. However, the fact that her book is titled and its cover vividly illustrated with the classical images of the mermaid and minotaur speaks compellingly to the immediacy and archetypal essence of these figures.

Beatrice Phillpotts' (1980) book entitled *Mermaids* is a fascinating inquiry into the lore and historical symbolism of this figure. Notably, Phillpotts is not a Jungian scholar, so her orientation, while steeped in recognition of the symbolic nutriment of the mermaid, does not draw the mermaid forth into the psychic landscape. Given the specificity and eternal nature of this image, the exploration of some of the foundational works surrounding the myth of the mermaid feels pertinent to the very nature of this inquiry. Intriguingly, Phillpotts began to extrapolate meaning from beyond the figure of the mermaid herself, and towards an understanding that it is her essential watery essence that amplifies the archetypal resonance of this mythological entity.

> The Sirens of today claim a long and rich ancestry that dates back to a multitude of fish tailed gods and goddesses of some of man's earliest civilizations. The sea, as womb of creation and the source of unfathomable wisdom, has always played an important role in world beliefs, particularly among maritime nations. The Gods of the Sea are among some of the most powerful in history, and their strength lives on in a host of submarine beings symbolic of the shifting, ever changing, dual nature of the sea as both life-giver and destroyer. (p. 7)

For Phillpotts, mermaids encapsulate a divided nature—an amalgam of worlds and states of opposing forces. To that end, it is important to elucidate the ways in which mermaids—and their original native realm of the sea—are also associated with this "dual nature . . . as both life-giver and destroyer." To the extent that mermaid physiognomy is a dazzling interpolation of animal and human, her psychological essence is also one of vibrant duality. The long arm of psychic memory leads from the mermaid to the siren, notably vengeful and desirous of seducing seafaring men to their watery depths. But, as Phillpotts revealed, the history and mythology of the mermaid is different and intensely conflictual: she both protects *and* destroys, sacrifices *and* murders.

Mermaid as Archetype

The image of the mermaid exists on the axis between the psychoidal, which can be defined as a "transpersonal realm of autonomous energy beyond the personal psyche" (Wikman, 2004, p. xvii) and the alchemical realms; the chthonic forces of the mythic and the archetypal are intertwined in this image. When an image is able to constellate and provide a sinew of connectivity between such ancient and numinous qualities and crossroads of experience, it is my sense that an archetypal encounter has been made. The concept of the *archetype* is complex and elusive. Jung (1954/1969a), Hollis (2000),

Hillman (1972, 1975, 1991), Eliade (1952/1991), and Singer (1994) have all made vast contributions to the dimensions of understanding that this particular word engenders. Archetypes, like mermaids, are "bipolar dynamic structures combining opposites within themselves" (Kalsched, 1996, p. 92) which cannot truly be seen, although they may indeed be experienced and even, perhaps to an extent, "witnessed."

> For Jung, all archetypes are bipolar dynamic structures combining opposites within themselves. One pole of the archetype represents *instinct* and related *affects* rooted in the body; the other pole is represented by a form-giving *spiritual* component made up of images produced by the mind. The *psyche* exists between these two opposites and represents a "third" factor combining instinct/affect and spirit into *unconscious fantasies* that create *meaning*. (Kalsched, 1996, p. 92)

Most succinctly, Jung defined an archetype as a "primordial image" (Jung, 1959/1968). Singer continued this gossamer thread of understanding by explaining that "since [archetypes] are unconscious, we cannot observe them directly, but we can see their manifestation everywhere about us in the form of archetypal images and symbols" (1994, p. 133). Essentially, what Jung as well as the coterie of post-Jungian analysts all convey through this archetypal, imaginal, mythopoetic lens is that archetypes can only be expressed through form or image. "Jung's archetypes are a dynamic and not just a formal reality, and the ideas and images in consciousness that reveal and conceal the archetypes are as real as the archetypes themselves" (Romanyshyn, 2007, p. 42). Like an inextricable archetypal double helix, the study of mermaids is indeed the study of two interpenetrating, highly complex psychological phenomenon: the anima and the archetype.

> The representations of the anima in Greek mythology, where the archetype appears in the configuration of nymphs, maenads, amazons, nereids, and so on, or in the more numinous and articulated divine forms of Persephone-Kore, Aphrodite, Artemis, Hebe, Athena, refer to a *structure of consciousness* relevant to the lives of both men and women. (Hillman, 1972, p. 50)

Essentially, Hillman was identifying that the anima is embodied archetypally within feminine mythological entities such as "nymphs . . . nereids, and so on" (p. 50). While Hillman did not include mermaids specifically within this description of mythological anima-embodiments, he certainly did make reference to the specific lineage of the feminine sea goddess ("nereids"), the psychical ancestors of the mermaid. This is where the relationship between the shadow and the anima begins to be elucidated. The mermaid shares a specific psychic proximity to the shadow as Jung identified the archetype of the anima as "the one standing closest behind the shadow" and that this archetype "is endowed with considerable powers of fascination and possession" (1954/1969b, p. 270 [*CW* 9i, para. 485]). The phenomenology of the archetype of the mermaid is indeed complex and dynamic. This is a border figure that exists at the crossroad of archetype, anima embodiment, and correspondingly, shadow. The shadow aspect, in particular, will be more comprehensively explored within the section entitled *Thanatos and the Mermaid*.

Mermaid Physiognomy: The Tail

Mermaids have the tail of a fish; this is a meaningful and essential aspect of their being. The symbol of the tail is important and will be explored symbolically in its relationship to our own intrapsychic development in terms of our inferior functions and shadow contents. This "integration of the tail, the inferior, those shadow aspects of self and life . . . which one drags around as one plows on ahead through life" (Wikman, 2004, p. 270) is a significant dimension of the archetypal transmission of the image of the mermaid, and will be mined for its depth psychological meaning. Von Franz gave voice to the allegorical potency of the tail: "Unless the head has integrated the tail, there is nothing" (as cited in Lao, 1998/2007, p. 176). In many ways, the tail is synechdocally symbolic of the shadow, the unconscious content that is nonetheless alive within each of us. Although different for each of us, it is the tail that perhaps we most share a disdain for—this phantom aspect of self that we have collectively severed from our acculturated and sanitized ego states. And herein exists yet another instance of the "split" that the mermaid encodes, for it is our "tail aspect" that roots us in that which is true and wild. Jung spoke to this potentiating aspect when he explained that "consciousness is continually widened through the confrontation with previously unconscious contents, or—to be more accurate—could be widened if we took the trouble to integrate them" (1957/1969, p. 91 [*CW* 8, para. 193]). The image of the mermaid is *precisely* this sort of confrontation with our own tail, our shadow, our unintegrated aspects of Self, the archaic and primitive remnants that despite our best conscious attempts, mobilize and animate with profound autonomy and personal implication. Lao, too, spoke to the psychoanalytic underpinning of this archaic aspect of self: "And lastly, there are the considerable psychoanalytic implications attached to the fish, for the Freudian Roheim, for example, the fusiform tail is a powerful phallic symbol, and the sirens, by exhibiting a tail-penis when the male expects to see a vulva, become the image of a phallic woman" (1998/2007, p. 124). While Roheim's assertion may certainly be congruent with a Freudian interpretation of the mermaid, Lao researched and iterated multiple possibilities other than the notion of mermaid-as-phallic-woman. As a counterpoint, for example, Lao identified the mermaid as a symbol of a fluid and feminine in-between-ness, having a "luminous and at the same time, dark character, the innermost aspect of the feminine" (p. 126): a mediatrix between realms, sexual orientation, and identities. This erotic disorientation will be further elaborated on within the section entitled *Beauty and the Beast: Mermaids and Eros*. When in the realm of the primitivity associated with a tail, there is a uroboric relational quality to alchemy that immediately reveals itself, and as such, mermaid-as-elemental is inherently charged with alchemical significance.

Mermaids *in Situ*: The Symbolism of Water

> In your waters we do not drown, but discover reflections which add depth to our experience.
>
> Downing, 2007, p. 203

It is significant that mermaids are creatures of water; water has powerful symbolic value. "The sea is the symbol of the unfathomable depth of the unconscious, or in mystical language, of the depth of the Godhead" (von Franz, 2006, p. 155). The life principle within Undine, and all mermaids, is *water*—deeply symbolic of the unconscious and of feminine mutability:

> Wells, springs, rivers, and lakes were sacred places in many cultures. Sacred waters are traditionally haunted by a host of female spirits, white ladies, mermaids, fairies or Naiades suggesting the submerged memory of a goddess. The water habitat symbolizes the fluid nature of female sexuality, and its ancient connections to water. (Mann & Lyle, 1995, p. 153)

As is Nature, the mermaid is transgressive, and as such, she transmutes instinctively, unconsciously, and divinely. Additionally, water is the symbol for baptism, spiritual rebirth, and renewal. It is also the primordial genesis from which all life originally hails: the psychic and physical *prima materia*, meaning "'first matter' or source of all creation" (Wikman, 2004, p. 42). So too it symbolizes the womb and the Great Mother archetype—both the benevolent creative as well as the darker destructive forces. Water can create and destroy, as we see in natural disasters such as floods, tsunamis, and drownings.

Congruent with the characterology of the mermaid, water itself epitomizes the cycle of creation and destruction and symbolizes renewal *and* annihilation, no less.

> In point of fact, the leap into the sea, more than any other physical event, awakens echoes of a dangerous and hostile initiation. It is the only, exact, reasonable image, the only image that can be experienced of a leap into the unknown. It is the sea, the womb, and the grave—all places of birth, rebirth, and regeneration where the enigma of transformation is concealed. The danger of the seduction of the sea becomes a metaphor for the womb, the grave, and the dangers of the feminine realm. (Bachelard, as cited in Lao, p. 34)

Paradoxically, as with all water elementals, mermaids embody a primal co-mingling of opposing energies, and as such, they can be as much an agent of good as evil, of self or other—precisely due to their dual and polytropic nature. This is a psyche that has scarcely left the natural world. The figure of the mermaid, like the beauty and grace of Nature even at its most tempestuous and destructive, must endure a constant and signally unconscious cycle of creation and destruction that she herself *generates.* "Metaphorically, water is the unconscious and the creature in the water is the life or energy of the unconsciousness, which has overwhelmed the conscious personality and must be disempowered, overcome and controlled" (Campbell with Moyers, 1988, p. 146). This reality—the figure of the mermaid as an agent of the natural and elemental world—creates an inescapable linkage between the realm of nature and its seeming divinely sanctioned lawlessness and the unconsciousness of, at least, *half* of this particular creature. Once again, James Hillman captured this intersecting point of consciousness and instinctual natural unconsciousness in a discussion of the relationship between the anima and the shadow—a richly fertile ground for this particular feminine aspect:

> She mystifies, produces sphinxlike riddles, prefers the cryptic and the occult where she can remain hidden: she insists upon uncertainty. By leading whatever is known from off its solid footing, she carries every question into deeper waters,

> which is also a way of soul-making. . . . Anima consciousness clings to unconsciousness, as the nymphs adhere to their dense wooden trees. (1991, p. 89)

In other words, mermaids (as perhaps do all goddesses) constellate the anima and bring secret, lost wisdom from the depths of the unconscious (water) and function to lure the active energies of the conscious mind into these uncharted unconscious realms.

Beauty and the Beast: Eros and the Mermaid

> The living experience of the Self is a monstrosity. It is a coming together of the opposites that appalls the ego and exposes it to anguish, demoralization, and violation of all reasonable considerations. *That's what a monstrosity is—a violation of everything we've come to expect as natural and reasonable and normal* [emphasis added]. (Edinger, 1995, p. 136)

Mermaids are split creatures. The waist of the mermaid is where the upper body of spirit and consciousness joins the lower pelvic realms of feminine sexuality. This physical lacuna is mirrored in their psychical and symbolic dichotomies: fish and woman, seductress and nurturing *inspiratrice*, murderer and savior, cultural consciousness and feminine primitivity. Mermaids utterly capture Edinger's definition of a "monstrosity" in that their cleaved and bifurcated nature repels all that we have come to viscerally recognize as "natural and reasonable and normal" (p. 136). What is to be made of this timeless, although perhaps unconscious, fascination with feminine "monstrosity"? What does the fact that mermaids exist at the far edge of otherness mean in terms of the collective relationship to the chthonic feminine? And how does our individual liminal recognition of our own primordial yet enduring chasm find voice and reflection within this archetype?

At best, mermaids have an elusive relationship to feminine sexuality; theirs is indeed a duplex nature with radically different states of "above" and "below." The majority of mermaid iconography depicts the mermaid sans genitalia, her sexuality usurped by the seamless vibrance of her sinewy—and nearly always nude—body. Intriguingly and significantly, it is perhaps precisely this lack of sexual demarcation that only serves to reify the collective recognition of the mermaid as a seductress, a sex symbol. In her book *Eros the Bittersweet*, internationally acclaimed author, poet, classicist, and university professor Anne Carson explained that "the Greek word *eros* denotes 'want,' 'lack,' 'desire for what is missing.' The lover wants what he does not have" (1998, p. 10). The Delphian figure of the mermaid *embodies* this purported and mysterious lack, "irradiating the absence whose presence is demanded by eros" (p. 16). Thus, we begin to see how mermaids lurk in a complex, primordial forcefield of repulsion and attraction, heightening the interplay between seduction and danger, shadow and light—yes and no—for she is a shape-shifter. "All human desire is poised on an axis of paradox, absence and presence its poles, love and hate its motive energies" (p. 11). As cultural theorist and professor Efrat Tseëlon captured, the imago of the mermaid activates something deeply complex and ancient within the human psyche: a recognition of our own reptilian ancestry, a beckoning towards love and death, and a specific amalgam of erotic stirring:

> And if her origin positions the mermaid between man and woman, fish and bird, her essence places her between a person, an animal, and a supernatural being, and between love and death (seduction and danger). Paradoxically, the impossibility of satisfying the desire she provokes is inscribed into her body, her tail. Her cosmological anomaly pre-figures her present-day alignment with the enigma of the woman caught up between conflicting images of nature and culture, seduction and nurturing, evil and holiness. (1995, para. 9)

Lao further explored the meaning of this imposed interruption of longing and the stunted erotic seduction symbolized by these enchantresses:

> In most cases, however, the siren is a sex symbol that lacks the essential organ. What is the meaning of this contradiction? Is it an example of their ambiguous

> nature? Or has the siren become another casualty of man's anxiety towards the female sex? (1998/2007, p. 133)

The "nature" of the mermaid is eternal: she is at once a compound and incomplete creature—half beast, half woman. The voluptuous instability (Clark, 1984, p. 273) of her very form seduces our mind into suspending our rational faculties and invites entrance into the realm of erotic imagination; in other words, her "triumphant artifice is subordinate to a poetic purpose" (p. 293). The nakedness of her upper body is often replete with splendid breasts (breasts themselves of course being a conflictual symbol of both maternal nourishment *and* erotic desire) which serve to potentially arouse and invite a sexual and erotic desire that her lower regions remain physically unable to fulfill; for Lao, she is once again a profoundly embodied paradox:

> Even for men free of religious preconceptions, the Sirens continue to represent the dark lady and must be imagined as creatures whose upper bodies awaken a desire that their lower parts are incapable of satisfying—the metaphor of the impenetrable feminine made literal. As always, they are objects of attraction and anguish, but now an additional level of mystery is added: wondering whether they possess female genitalia is more troubling than knowing either way. Whatever the case, whether in excess or lacking, virtual or real, a new, disturbing sexuality is now attributed to the Sirens. (1998/2007, p. 135)

In all aspects, mermaids exist on the plane of enchanted unreality and duplexity. Our mind continues to reach for an answer to the fundamental erotic dilemma, the physical and psychical ambiguity she encapsulates. It is precisely this polytropic nature that allows the symbol of the mermaid to break through planes of consciousness and penetrate mythologically and psychically into realms far beyond its essential form. There is a reason for this transcendent facility, for the mermaid functions as a spiritual symbol (Eliade, 1952/1991).

The Symbol of the Mermaid

Throughout this thesis, mermaids have been referred to as a "symbol" or reference has been made to their "symbolic" value. Within the tradition of depth psychology, the notion of the symbol has rich nutriment and meaning. The meaning of the term *symbol* is signally important to understanding the potency of the archetypal dimension of the image of the mermaid. Jung and many post-Jungian analysts have written extensively on the complexity and psychological marrow of this word. Many postmodern and post-structural writers have also engaged deeply with the semiotic significance of this word within our modern culture and experience of Self. Eliade began to illuminate the spiritual function of the symbol when he explained that

> the symbol reveals certain aspects of reality—the deepest aspects—which defy any other means of knowledge. Images, symbols, and myths are not irresponsible creations of the psyche; they respond to a need and fulfill a function, that of bringing to the light the most hidden modalities of being. (1952/1991, p. 12)

Following Eliade's premise, the symbol of the mermaid remains an essentially unwavering mythological, intrapsychic, and cultural figure precisely because she carries transcendent meaning; the figure of the mermaid functions on multiple, wholly paradoxical, and yet symbolic levels. Eliade further elucidated that "all symbolism of transcendence is paradoxical, impossible to conceive on the profane level" (p. 83). The mermaid does not exist with the profane world; to encounter her requires a leap into the imaginal, symbolic, and mythological. The symbol of the mermaid evokes a psychological, archetypal, and symbolic *experience.* Jung explained the psychological significance of the symbol:

> The symbols aiming at wholeness . . . are the remedy with whose help [illness] can be repaired by restoring to the conscious mind a spirit and an attitude which from time immemorial have been felt as solving and healing in their effects. They

> are “représentations collectives” [collective images] that facilitate the much needed union of conscious and unconscious. This union cannot be accomplished either intellectually or in a purely practical sense because in the former case the instincts rebel and in the latter case reason and morality. . . . [T]he conflict can only be resolved through the symbol. . . . The synthesis of conscious and unconscious can only be implemented by a conscious confrontation with the latter, and this is not possible unless one understands what the unconscious is saying. During this process we come upon the symbols . . . and in coming to terms with them we reestablish the lost connection with ideas and feelings that make a synthesis of the personality possible. (1948/1969, p. 191 [*CW* 11, para. 285])

In a compelling example of the potent incongruity that mermaids embody and engender, here we discern that the two somatic aspects of the mermaid correspond, metaphorically speaking, to the conscious (woman) and unconscious (animal) realms of our intrapsychic experience. According to Jung, it is precisely a “conscious confrontation” with the symbol that facilitates a “synthesis of the personality” (p. 191 [*CW* 11, para. 285]). The psychical essence and physiognomy of the mermaid speak to this archetypal engagement with pristine alacrity and symbolism; the mermaid is a symbolic portrayal of our timeless psychic processes, realities, and mysteries. Jung (1954/1969a) described archetypes as “universal images that have existed since the remotest times” (p. 5 [*CW* 9i, para. 5]). He theorized that an archetype is “a collective image, common to a time or a culture, a crystalline shape to which art and myth give form” (1921/1971, p. 443). Symbols and archetypes mean something; like images, they speak to the psyche, they speak the language of the soul. Liberation psychologist, noted author, and core faculty member at Pacifica Graduate Institute Mary Watkins described how Psyche “speaks” a language of images and reveals herself “in the form of images, for that is her experience. If we wish to befriend her, to love her, we must take great care how we react to her, life speaks itself to us” (1984, p. 56). So too, through the symbol of the mermaid, “life speaks itself to us.” Embedded more deeply within the mythological symbol of the mermaid is the fact that she functions not only as symbol and archetype, but fluently consolidates Jung's (1936/1968) alchemical principle of the *coincidentia oppositorum*. In other words, the mermaid functions as a uniting symbol of various archetypal, symbolic, and as we shall see, select alchemical processes. However, this symbol notably is not a "coniunctio" imago, as her nature is exclusively feminine (albeit chthonic)—she lacks all traces of the masculine principle.

Coincidentia Oppositorum: Mermaids and Alchemy

> The self is made manifest in the opposites and in the conflict between them; it is a *coincidentia oppositorum*. Hence the way to the self begins with conflict.
>
> Jung, 1936/1968, p. 186 [*CW* 12, para. 259]

While there are many alchemical implications within the symbol of the elemental mermaid and specifically within the mermaid character of *Undine,* the principle of *coincidentia oppositorum* will be addressed within this discourse. *Coincidentia oppositorum* is a Latin phrase meaning "coincidence of opposites" (Eliade, 1976). The symbol of the mermaid is ultimately a symbol of unity—but requires the juxtaposition and "coincidence" of opposing forces in order to arrive at this symbiosis of paradox. This convergence of opposing forces has multifold psychological implications and clinical applications; this chasm is built into the very foundation of Self:

> The capacity to make room in unconsciousness for different parts of us, different points of view, to sit, hold, and contemplate, helps build what Jung calls the transcendent function, the bridge-building between opposites that lays the foundation for new attitudes that can both include and surpass the old. (Ulanov & Ulanov, 2004, p. 118)

Here, the husband and wife team of Barry Ulanov, mid-century scholar, theologian, and Barnard professor and his wife, Ann, noted Jungian analyst and author (2004) begin to speak to the transcendent aspect that is constellated when we are able to hold the tension between the opposing forces and appetites of the Self. The notion of the transcendent function as a "bridge" between conscious and unconscious, old and new is a specific psychological underpinning of the symbolic function of the mermaid. Jung expounded on the healing function of the symbol of united duality in the following explanation:

> Just as conscious as well as unconscious phenomena are to be met with in practice, the self as psychic totality also has a conscious as well as an unconscious aspect. Empirically, the self appears in dreams, myths, and fairy tales in the figure of the supraordinate personality . . . such as a king, hero, prophet, savior, etc., or in the form of a totality symbol, such as the circle, square, quadratura circuli, etc. When it represents a complexio oppositorum, a union of opposites, it can also appear as a united duality, in the form, for instance, of tao as the interplay of yang and yin, or of the hostile brothers, or of the hero and his adversary (arch-enemy, dragon), Faust and Mephistopheles, etc. Empirically, therefore, the Self appears as a play of light and shadow, although conceived as a totality and unity in which the opposites are united. Since such a concept is irrepresentable . . . it is transcendental on this account also. It would, logically considered, be a vain speculation were it not for the fact that it designates symbols of unity that are found to occur empirically. *(1921/1971, p. 481 [CW6, paras. 789-791])*

The mermaid is a spiritual symbol that serves to function as a "psychic totality" and through her embodied paradox, carries the vital archaic forces and animal impulses that are deeply buried but remain very much alive in our collective—and personal—psyches. The alchemical symbol of the mermaid speaks directly to our instinctive nature and, century after century, celebrates this thrust of instinct against our increasingly distanced sphere of human consciousness. According to Jung (1921/1971), Eliade (1976), and the Ulanovs (2004), this sort of psychic aliveness and transcendence is paradoxical and impossible to make contact with within the strata of the profane; it requires making contact with the archaic and archetypal dimensions of the psyche. The mermaid remains alive in the collective consciousness and human culture precisely because she carries psychoactivating content in the form of the *coincidentia oppositorum* that is spontaneously recognized by the psyche. It is significant that her image within our culture has been unilaterally depotentiated. Her iconic form has been infantilized in the form of Ariel (from Disney's incarnation of *The Little Mermaid* film (Musker & Ashman, Clements & Musker, 1989) and storybooks) and sanitized in the form of Barbie Mermaid; it is likely that our animus-possessed collective psyche can only bear small sips of the chthonic inter-psychic messaging that "she" transmits through her embodied dichotomy.

> As Jung saw it, the mystery of the divine Self within each of us forms in the flow of energy between polarities, or opposites, where conscious and unconscious meet. Spirit and instinct are a central pair of polarities between which psychic energy flows. Opposites define each other; they are dynamic polarities reflecting a mysterious oneness. There is not one without the other. (Wikman, 2004, p. 28)

Despite her depotentiation, her presence—albeit diluted—within our contemporary culture speaks to the fact that we remain enlivened by her chthonic pulse.

> For the unconscious is not haunted by monsters alone: the gods, the goddesses, the heroes, and the fairies dwell there too: moreover, the monsters of the unconscious are themselves mythological, seeing that they continue to fulfill the same functions that they fulfilled in in all the mythologies—in the last analysis, that of helping man to liberate himself, to complete his initiation. (Eliade, 1952/1991, p. 14)

Eliade too saw the psychoanalytic vitality of her presence: the mermaid beckons to us from her watery underworld to "liberate" ourselves, and the ensoulment she encounters within her mythological vestiges is a spontaneous rediscovery of our own call towards initiatory experiences, a remembering. Eliade referred to the *coincidentia oppositorum* as "the mythical pattern" (1976, p. 449) and further identified the potency of this phenomena within "the very nature of divinity, which shows itself, by turns or even simultaneously, benevolent and terrible, creative and destructive, solar and serpentine, and so on (in other words, actual and potential)" (1976, p. 449).

Similarly, Lao recognized the collisional form of mermaids ("Sirens") as a way of conveying the profoundly conflictual yet cosmological nature of that which is internal versus external, the spiritual versus the corporeal, and the metaphysical (unconscious) versus the natural (conscious):

> In alchemy . . . the Sirens were considered a positive symbol. As the union of fish (rising sulfur) and the virgin (common mercury), they embodied the philosophical mercury or salt of knowledge. Above all, the sirens connoted the supreme conjunction of opposites, the alchemical intention of rendering external that which is internal, spiritual that which is corporeal, metaphysical that which is natural. (1998/2007, p. 122)

Thanatos and The Mermaid

> Nature is sometimes harsh, severe, and cruelly revengeful. There is neither judgement nor rule, but the revenge of the dark aspect of the feminine nature goddess.
>
> von Franz, 1993, p. 39

Mermaids have long been associated with death. Her older winged sisters, the sirens, were thought to be succubaes luring the heroic seafaring man to his death with her dazzling sonorous beckoning. This timeless instinct is illuminated quite potently within the gothic and tragic tale of *Undine* (de la Motte Fouque, 1814/2002). A summary of the story follows within Chapter III, but it concludes with Knight Huldbrand, Undine's beloved husband, dying in her arms of her sublime yet murderous embrace. Despite the overt travesty, this action illuminates both an archetypal dimension as well as an intrinsic *logos*. Undine, a water sprite (though never appended with a tail), is an elemental entity. She remains close to the primitive uprushing of Nature. And so, when her beloved husband, the symbolic embodiment of acculturated consciousness, defied the natural laws that had been bestowed upon him during his marriage to the chthonic entity of Undine, revenge—perhaps justice—was required to restore the cosmological and mythological Order of Things. Von Franz brilliantly illuminated this inherent function within her book, *The Feminine in Fairy Tales*:

> Certain rules have to be made and those who do not keep them must be punished. . . . But there is another process of revenge and punishment which I would like to define as the *revengefulness of nature*. . . . It cannot be called a legal punishment; it is a natural consequence—wrong behavior is followed by bad luck or illness. (1993, p. 39)

To understand this sort of Thanatos instinct, it becomes necessary to emancipate ourselves from our Western cultural morality and to recognize the fierce feminine impulse that dwells within anima and Nature alike; there is a certain attribute of nastiness implicit within anima and Nature, for each constellate the primitive (von Franz, 1993). This death instinct can be identified within goddesses such as Kali and draw upon an understanding of the cosmological relationship between life and death, creation and destruction. Both *Undine* as well as the *The Little Mermaid* touch deeply into this aspect of the mermaid phenomenology. It is a vital dimension of the mermaid's relatedness to archetypal significance, and needs to be differentiated from a sanguinary impulse. Jung identified this primitive anima/animal nature within the unconsciousness of the mermaid:

> The nixie is an even more instinctive version of a magical feminine being whom I call the *anima*. She can also be a siren, *melusina* (mermaid), wood-nymph, Grace, or Erlking's daughter, or a lamia or succubus, who infatuates young men and sucks the life out of them. (1954/1969a, p. 25 [*CW* 9i, para. 55])

Concluding Remarks

> The imaginal is entered primarily through interested love; it is a creation of faith, need, and desire.
>
> Hillman, 1972, p. 86

The mermaid is a mythic, fish-tailed enchantress that is evocative of complex archetypal content. Mermaids dwell in the place in the psyche where instinct finds its images; they embody an inner psychic reality that can only be expressed in a symbol. The symbol of the mermaid is a diptych of sorts, an embodiment of the irrational aspects of human nature and the vestiges of animal impulse. Thus far, the symbol of the mermaid has been explored at the level of an archetype and within the plane of the psychoidal. The next chapter will introduce the fairy tale entitled *Undine* by Frederich de la Motte Fouque (1814/2002) as well as *The Little Mermaid* (Andersen, 1837/1976). It is Undine herself, a potent elemental *inspiratrice*, who has led me on this journey towards a reclamation of the submerged feminine. Within this initiatory tale of emerging consciousness unravels an archetypal story of the underworld: alchemy, love, betrayal, dark spirit-laden forests, and death. Using von Franz's (1996) approach to exploring the dramatic structure of the story, the symbolic meaning of specific story attributes will then be explored through an archetypal psychological perspective. It is not my intention, however, to remain fully within the parameters of a theoretical orientation. More so, it is a grateful and curious exploration of the shadow *and* soul-making (i.e., "angel aspect") (Hillman, 1975, p. 9) paradox that is very much alive and encoded within the symbol of the mermaid.

Chapter III
The Descent

Mermaids invite one into the depths, into our depths. The symbol of the mermaid is saturated with complex and archaic influences, yet is psychologically nimble and remains very much alive within our cultural and collective landscape. I have been living with the symbol of the mermaid for over a year and have followed her beneath the world as we know it into her watery precincts. In spite of the extensive time spent in her symbolic and mythological realms, I have only recently begun to understand the archetypal dynamics behind my relationship to the mermaid. This has required deepening the relationship between my conscious perspective (and at times, my conscious understanding) and leaning more trustingly into the archetypal scaffolding upon which this relationship exists. I recognize, of course, that the symbol of the mermaid is a wholly psychological event. I also am aware that the image of the mermaid is a *living* symbol, and part of the world in which I live.

She is alive for me.

There are times when I very much connect with a certain *joie de vivre* that the symbol of the mermaid connotes, but more often, it is her timeless sorrow that more profoundly resonates for me. Through (and with) the mermaids, I have come to understand that I have been seeking a truth—perhaps my truth—one that is inwardly transforming and serves as a source of renewal and recognition: I would now call this principle "the feminine." It feels important to illuminate that by "feminine," I am not referring to a woman or a girl, but a phenomenon and archetypal sub-structure of consciousness. I am referring to a quality of experience that can perhaps be felt through ways of being that include a non-linearity—a receptive, feeling, instinctive mode. Notably, this is not mutually exclusive from an intellectual rigor and analytical prowess—but the *process* is intrinsically different. The feminine comes alive at night, under a luminescent moon and alongside the sensual bloom of night jasmine. It whispers and undulates, tastes of blood and *fleur de sel*, and is birthed in the waters of the unconscious. To differentiate its qualities further, a masculine phenomenology can be described as solar, fast, linear, and penetrating. The feminine can easily be confused with artifacts or *fantasies* of the feminine: inflated lips and breasts, a painted pout; I can't help but wonder if these overt and often enhanced *signifiers* of a physically idealized femininity are perhaps a compensatory function of losing contact with the Goddess mythologies and rituals:

> If a god is forgotten, it means that some aspects of collective consciousness are so much in the foreground that others are ignored to a great extent. The archetype of the mother goddess has suffered that fate in our civilization. (von Franz, 1993, p. 30)

This is perhaps more complex and intricate than it initially appears. Von Franz was likely referring to a predominance of masculine or patriarchal consciousness within the collective. The compensatory function to which I am referring is constellated by a masculine *projection* of the idealized feminine attributes associated with goddess incarnations. Marilyn Monroe comes to mind as an iconic example of a mortal goddess incarnation. Quite often, when a human carries that sort of collective archetypal activation, the *human* life is inevitably tragic.

This theoretical and psychological immersion via "re-search" into the symbol of the mermaid has served to awaken in me a conscious longing for the reclamation of the feminine, one that, unlike the version of feminine consciousness I have "inherited" from family and culture, is a *remembrance* and a *return* to authentic embodied feeling.

> Research as re-search has, therefore, a different orientation. As a work of mourning, its first direction is not forward into new areas of knowledge. Rather, its first move is backwards, towards what has been lost, forgotten, or left behind. As a work of mourning, research as re-search is a work of anamnesis, which advances by remembering. It moves forward by stepping backwards to regard, recover, redeem, and renew what has been left behind, and in this orientation it opens a space for a new beginning. Re-search with soul in mind thus transforms what we uncritically take for granted by returning to origins for the sake of an *other* beginning. (Romanyshyn, 2007, pp. 76-77)

The mermaid and her watery underworld have demanded of me a recognition: a glimpse of psychic wholeness seen through the sylvan forest of Undine's childhood home, a tiny remembrance espied in the little mermaid's lush, underworld garden. Their story has become my story, so that I might remember, so that I might find my way to self:

> Fairy tales, myths, and stories provide understandings which sharpen our sight so that we can pick out and pick up the path. . . . The instruction found in story reassures us that the path has not run out, but still leads women deeper, and more deeply still, into their own knowing. (Estés, 1992, p. 6)

Her story is my story.

Unlike any other image or archetypal encounter I have known before, the image of the mermaid has required a descent, leading me more deeply towards my sense of self, at times leaving me gasping for breath when I have been lost in her watery underworld:

> One must only adhere firmly to one's own inner experience, without exteriorizing it uselessly, and also without denying it. If this numinous experience is accepted with sincerity, genuineness, and courage, it will bring forth a conversion, a "metamorphosis," a profound transformation of one's entire being. (von Franz, 1992, p. 196)

The mermaids have taught me to listen to and witness their story, and most importantly, to be attentive to the *whole*. The symbol of the mermaid demands this recognition and engagement, as she is not fish *or* woman but fish *and* woman. The mermaid is a chimerical creature—her body is half-animal. Through dreams and reverie, I have felt this aspect of her being in highly somaticized and visceral ways—most notably, by waking with my legs aching from being tightly bound within a fish's tail the night before in my dreams. Throughout the entire day, my legs ached . . . similarly to the little mermaid, there was pain with each step I took. I realize now how alive and excruciating this process of reclaiming the feminine has been for me; that as there was pain with each physical step, so too has there been psychical pain with each step closer I have drawn to the sense of loss and grief this image has constellated.

> Images also come that aren't quite so beautiful as flowers. . . . They make us face the other side of ourselves. The point is we are flesh and blood and often we don't experience the reality of a psychic image until we feel it in our body. (Woodman, 1993, p. 118)

I realized when reading the words of von Franz, the relationship I have with the image of the mermaid is *actually kinetic*; I *feel* her. I long for the tail that forces me to connect in more instinctive and embodied ways with the world around me, that allows me to swim more deeply in the unconscious waters. And, yet, I also remain grateful for the human legs that allow me to walk on land towards a greater consciousness. The tail is vital; this animal aspect cannot be forgotten by either body or psyche.

Von Franz discussed the symbolic meaning of animals in fairy tales within the arc of the redemptive process at great length. She wrote,

> It becomes clear what cursing a human being by transforming it into an animal really means: it is a mistake, an overbalance towards the body pole, i.e.: the infra-red pole. Something which should be lived more in the psychic or spiritual field is obliged to be lived on the animal pattern. (1980, p. 53)

Von Franz specifically identified the symbolic marrow that is transmitted via the artifact of the mermaid's tail through her recognition that "something which should be lived more in the psychic or spiritual field is obliged to be lived on the animal pattern" (p. 53). In other words, that which the mermaid carries physically is not yet able to be integrated consciously or "spiritually" and therefore must remain incarnated within the animal plane. The mermaid's tail is a symbol of our displaced and perhaps undeveloped sense of instinctual, embodied, authentic feeling: the feminine principle. In this light, the mermaid can be seen as a reflection of our cultural, psychical, and for me, personal relationship to the lost, hidden, or displaced feminine nature. Woodman spoke to this process of extrojecting this "inner image of femininity" (1992, p. 1) onto such creatures as a "sphinx, or a dragon" (p. 2); I would theorize that this canon of mythological creatures would likely include the nymph, the fairy, as well as the mermaid:

> For centuries, men have projected their inner image of femininity, raising it to a consciousness that left women who accepted the projection separated from their own reality. They became artifacts rather than people. The consciousness attributed to them was a consciousness projected onto them. That projection was sometimes an idealized image of beauty and truth, a sphinx, or a dragon. Whatever it was, it could not be an incarnated woman. (pp. 1-2)

Notably, Woodman captured the masculine aspect of this psychic phenomenon via her recognition that this projection occurs within the realm of "men"; however, I very much sense that there is an intrapsychic dimension to this phenomenology, and that this projection readily occurs within the animus-possessed collective psyche of the modern woman. I have an intimate relationship with this hypothesis, as it is very much the essence of my psychic process.

Intriguingly, within a later lecture, von Franz cited an example where God teaches all the little water creatures ancient medicine rituals and secrets *rather* than the human beings. Von Franz explained that

> they have to learn through the instinctual movements of the body which is what we try to do in analysis when we ask people to do active imagination and follow mainly physical instincts and impulses. . . . The first start has to be made through the body. (1980, p. 69)

In this case, it seems as though the embodied and animalistic "first start" (recalling that the people had to learn healing practices from the *animals*) is actually what *leads* a person entangled in neurosis towards the infra-violet or more spiritual/psychic aspect of themselves. This is a compelling dichotomy and question to me both within the landscape of fairy tale and psyche alike. How—and when—does this regressive yearning towards—or perhaps a more immediate encounter with—a more primal, archaic, animalistic infra-red pole/state of being actually *serve* redemption (in fairy tales) or the psyche's innate and intrinsic movement towards the infra-violet pole (i.e., psychic wellbeing) in analysis? These questions very much echo the originating questions that prompted the research into this thesis topic: How can we unite the most primitive and civilized aspects of Psyche within our own human existences? How can we hold the tension between the instinctive, erotic, unconscious aspect of the human psyche (i.e., the feminine principle) along with the civilized, refined, *logos*-saturated and conscious aspect of Self? How can we support our clients in making contact with this archaic and instinctual aspect of self? Is it possible to regulate this encounter within the analytic container?

Clinical Relevance of Fairy Tales

Fairy tales hold significant relevance to the therapeutic process in several ways.

Notably, when a client shares a dream, it is often immediately and potently evocative of a fairy tale. It is a realm in which creatures may abound, there is often a journey or odyssey, a confrontation or battle, something precious may be lost or found . . . whether it be the heart of the beloved, or a ring of green jasper in this "once upon a time" world between worlds. Much of this collective content and archetypal symbolism is woven through fairy tale and folklore and, as such, mobilizes a healing and transcendent function: we recognize and learn to remember the archaic and instinctual aspect of Self. Reading—and telling—our story opens us to our truth. "Fairy tales are the purest and simplest expressions of collective unconscious psychic processes" (von Franz, 1996, p. 1). As such, they reflect our foundational, invisible, intrapsychic contents, and allow us to experience the psychic objective reality of these images, entities, and metaphorical quests within the archetypal landscape of story. As an image-making entity, the psyche instinctively responds to symbols, and creates relationship between this psychic *prima materia* and outer-world physical or psychological elements. Fairy tales bridge the kingdom of the enchanted/imaginal and the conventional world in which we must walk. Though called dreams, the psyche itself is a nocturnal, fairy tale-producing instrument:

> Dreams either compensate for the lopsidedness of our conscious view or complement its lacunae. Fairy tales, because they are mostly unsophisticated products of the storyteller's unconscious, do the same. Like dreams, they help to keep our conscious attitude in a healthy balance, and therefore have a healing function. (von Franz, 1993, p. 10)

When we read a fairy tale, Psyche alights, recognizing—perhaps only unconsciously at first—the symbolic material of the collective unconscious. This is the world of archetypes and symbolism encoded within story, flight-of-fancy, and costume, and yet the unique distancing or distillation process that story provides often allows for a greater recognition or accessibility of Self. Like Narcissus, we see ourselves in these still waters; instinctively we know the quenching relief of seeing the first fragment of light as we emerge from a dark and mysterious forest, and pray that when we too are faced with a descent to the underworld, that we may carry with us a protective elixir or clever treat to keep the ferocious hounds at bay. Metaphors and symbolism course deeply within fairy tales, and reveal to us meaning, nutriment, and recognition of a deeper aspect of our own psychic substructure. Psyche, like fairy tales, “contains” and recognizes the collective unconscious, and just as in a dream, we can constellate many dimensions of archetypal reality: Grandma, Little Red Riding Hood, *and* the Big Bad Wolf, no less. To hold this understanding with our clients, to help them amplify their own symbolic language through the lens of fairy tale and the mythopoeic world, will (ideally) allow them a greater sense of Self and place within the magical world of story and within conventional—conscious—reality alike.

I come to life through the stories that I tell.

Unforgetting

Our earliest human beginnings are astonishingly similar: we grew from a miraculous cluster of cells within the watery world of the womb. Each of us began as a little fish creature, replete with tail and a tiny little organ of breathing: the gill. Chromosomally, each of us began as a female, male attributes blossoming only later in embryonic development. The image of the mermaid stirs our earliest cellular and amniotic memory: *we all begin as mermaids*. This physical reality has a psychical, archaic component. Even before our human incarnation, we emerged from the waters, our vestigial amphibian form learning to emerge from the waters and walk upon land. Of course, this corresponds metaphorically to our prehistoric evolution from unconsciousness towards consciousness. The mermaid is reflective of our archaic betwixt nature, her bicaudal tail harkening back to our primordial genesis, an artifact symbolizing both a physical and psychological primitivity.

> We were born of the water and lived in its realm for hundreds of years. Our extended transmutation from reptilian form to human form is reflected in the form of the mermaid. This metaphor resonates because it connects us to our watery roots and reminds us that the story is not yet done. (Felty, 2002)

There is a temporal fluidity encapsulated in the recognition that "the story is not yet done" that alights for me. The symbol of the mermaid paradoxically reveals our ancient, collective "watery roots" and yet, at the same time, serves as a portal, a totemic reminder to remember the instinctive aspect of self: the feminine principle. Eliade, too, spoke to this long arm of cellular personal and collective memory through his acknowledgment that "every man carries on, within himself, a great deal of prehistoric history" (1952/1991, p. 12). The image of the mermaid is one of mythological, cosmological, and evolutionary primitivity: a nude female torso fused with the tail of the fish. There is perhaps no greater symbolic embodiment of our psychic and ancestral roots and emergence as the mermaid.

We all begin as mermaids.

Correspondingly, there is a psychological and imaginal counterpoint to the idea of a "cellular memory" that is constellated by the image of the mermaid. Eliade captured this aspect of the life of the image as a longing for innocence, for Paradise. He explained that

> these images express the nostalgia for a mythicized past transformed into an archetype, and that this "past" signifies not only regrets for a vanished time, but countless other meanings . . . in short, the longing for something *altogether*

> *different* from the present instant; something in fact inaccessible or irretrievably lost: "Paradise" itself. (1952/1991, p. 17)

This idea very much resonated for me. I intrinsically recognize that despite the seductive and, at times, lethal framework in which the mermaid has been canonized, that paradoxically, she also very much constellates a state of feminine sexual innocence. This is perhaps most formally and semiotically introduced by the physical absence of womanly genitalia and notable frequent lack of motherhood. To that same end, the mermaid image presents as timelessly youthful; an aging or crone embodiment of the mermaid archetype remains entirely rare across cultures and time (although notably, the only maternal presence in the story of the little mermaid is her dowager paternal grandmother). In other words, *visually* the image of the mermaid corresponds to the *puella aeterna*—a Jungian term meaning "eternal girl" in Latin (Woodman, 1985, p. 192)—aspect of feminine psychic life. It is important to elucidate that a common aspect to the various myths and stories of the mermaid is very much one of incarnation as a (human) woman—but that other than the deeply significant transmutation of tail-into-legs, this incarnation occurs intrapsychically rather than within a physical transmutation. As is her true dual and conflictual nature, the symbol of the mermaid remains suspended within the girlish embodiment of a *puella aeterna,* although her intrapsychic development is more deeply congruent with a path of feminine individuation. Eliade touched on the ineffable and often tender unconscious longing that the image of the mermaid bestows upon us: "What is important about these images of the nostalgia for paradise is that they always express more than the subject who has experienced them could convey in words" (1952/1991, p. 17).

I experience this longing for innocence through the gnostic sensuality of my body.

It is very much my sense that while the image of the mermaid is indeed timeless, that she also functions as an ancient psychic relic. I have discussed the way that she cathects an encounter with our primordial beginnings, but I also sense that she has vestigial anachronistic qualities. *She doesn't belong here*, and yet each of her creative and commercial iterations (i.e., Disney's *The Little Mermaid* film (Musker & Ashman, Clements & Musker, 1989) with associated branded product extensions and the famed iconic mermaid within the Starbucks logo) is met with terrific fiscal and imagistic success. Why is this so? How is it that she stays "alive" within our collective psychic landscape?

> This was to forget that the life of modern man is swarming with half-forgotten myths, decaying hierophanies and secularized symbols. The progressive de-sacralization of modern man has altered the content of his spiritual life without breaking the matrices of his imagination: a quantity of mythological litter still lingers in the ill-controlled zones of his mind. (Eliade, 1952/1991, p. 18)

Eliade explained that the spiritual life of modern man is being categorically "desacralized" and that symbols, despite their depotentiation within our cultural matrix, remain alive within the more instinctual, primitive (i.e., "ill-controlled") aspects of our psyche. It is my conjecture that the symbol of the mermaid is precisely this sort of "mythological litter" that lingers within our psychic, biological, and ontological history. She functions as a link from who we are to who we were, and, as a singular example of a psychoperceptual symbolic event, serves to collapse the distinction between the two. She returns us to ourselves.

The symbol and the story of the mermaid reminds me of who I am.

Undine: A Brief Summary of the Novella

> It was the dark pool of the sound of the word that first took me: if our auditory imaginations were sufficiently tuned to plumb and sound a vowel, to unite the most primitive and civilized associations, "Undine" would probably suffice as a poem in itself.
>
> Seamus Heaney, 1981, p. 52

From a faraway place and time emerges the 19th century Germanic love story of Undine (de la Motte Fouque, 1814/2002). It is said that an enchanting and mysterious water nymph, herself the story's namesake, is endowed with soul only upon holy matrimony to a mortal man. Within this initiatory tale of emerging consciousness unravels an archetypal story of the underworld: alchemy, love, betrayal, dark, spirit-laden forests, and death.

Undine is the foster daughter of an old, pious fisherman and his wife, both of whom remain nameless throughout the novella. The story begins with the sudden arrival of Knight Huldbrand, who emerges from the deep shadows of the forest due to a tempestuous storm. Undine appears shortly after the Knight's arrival to her parents' humble fishing cottage. Undine is a water sprite who marries Knight Huldbrand to acquire a human soul. She later loses this human love because of the treacheries of her Uncle Kuhleborn and Lady Bertalda (de la Motte Fouque, 1814/2002).

After being reprimanded for her rather forward interaction with the knight, Undine, a plucky and impertinent girl, runs off into the darkness of the stormy evening, leaving her old father and their illustrious guest, Knight Huldbrand, fretting until the early morning hours. Upon discovering her safely, the knight and Undine begin a love affair, resulting in wedlock. The day after the wedding, Undine confesses to her beloved husband that she was indeed "a tender mermaid . . . an Undine" (de la Motte Fouque,

1814/2002, p. 42). Undine also discloses that her father was a "powerful water-prince in the Mediterranean Sea" (p. 43) and that her Uncle Kuhleborn was "powerful . . . and beloved by many streams; and, as he brought me hither to the fisherman, a light-hearted laughing child, he will take me back again to my parents, a loving, suffering, and soul-endowed woman" (p. 43).

The newly betrothed set off the next day through the dark forest for Sir Huldbrand's Imperial City accompanied by the priest, whereupon they encounter Undine's menacing Uncle Kuhleborn. Like Undine, her Uncle Kuhleborn is a multiplex creature: able to be embodied as man as well as natural water formations, most often of dangerous incarnations. They arrive safely in the Imperial City where Undine and Lady Bertalda, the previous love interest of the knight, become dear friends, each having the sense that they somehow know of one another. It becomes apparent, through the meddling of the omnipotent Uncle Kuhleborn, that a rather convoluted history exists between the two, and that Bertalda is indeed the long-lost daughter (presumed dead) of the pious fisherman and his wife. Bertalda rages against this seeming indignity, and is soothed only by Undine and the knight, who invite her along their journey down the Danube river (de la Motte Fouque, 1814/2002).

The knight experiences ongoing doubt and dismay over his wife's elemental nature. Undine pleads with her husband to honor only two things:

1. That he refrain from strong words with her when near or on the water, to prevent her subterranean relatives from seizing her from presumed mortal toil.
2. That he remain faithful to her and their sacred marriage.

Upon the boat sailing down the Danube with Bertalda, the knight lapses in his promise not to use harsh words or be angry with Undine when near or on the water, and as a result, the weeping Undine slips into the river, not to be seen in corporeal form again. After some time, Bertalda and Knight Huldbrand are set to marry, to the great dismay of their beloved old priest, Father Heilmann. Nonetheless, the wedding ensues and as a result, Undine is required to take the life of her beloved husband. According to the legend, she weeps him to death with her tears (de la Motte Fouque, 1814/2002).

It is intriguing to note that the story opens with a triumvirate of "worthy people": the Knight, the old fisherman, and his wife. Notably, there are two other figures: Undine and Uncle Kuhleborn, although neither are mortal (de la Motte Fouque, 1814/2002). The story ends at the funeral of Knight Huldebrand. The old woman, the foster-mother of Undine, has died. This may represent the absence of feminine wisdom, or perhaps could also signify the dying of the old feminine in order to create the new—very much one of the symbolic tropes of the tale. The Knight has also died—killed by Undine and her torrent of tears—representing perhaps the absence of the creative, regenerative masculine.

There are now two priests, one present at the funeral, and the original beloved Father Heilmann, who so dutifully warned the knight against his marriage to Lady Bertalda, and who remains in the proximity, but not at the funeral itself. And of course, Lady Bertalda is present at the funeral. Undine is there, too—although not in her mortal form, but as a white, vaporous figure, and then, coming to rest as a silvery spring upon her beloved husband's grave (de la Motte Fouque, 1814/2002).

The Little Mermaid: A Brief Summary

The story of the little mermaid begins "very deep, deeper than any anchor can reach" (Andersen, 1837/1976, p. 46) beneath the surface of the sea. It is a world where a powerful Sea King dwelled in his crystal palace with his six daughters and his "old mother," who "keeps house for him" (p. 46). Notably, the Sea King was a widower and as such, his six "sea-Princesses" (p. 46) were motherless. The youngest of the daughters, who was "curious . . . and thoughtful" (p. 47), longed only for "the world of humans up above the sea" (p. 47), and would beg her grandmother to tell her of the strange delights that existed in this other world . . . flowers that had scent, exotic little winged creatures that could fly, and trees of green. This littlest mermaid's grandmother assured her, as she had for each of her sisters, that upon her 15th birthday, she too would permitted to "rise to the surface, and to sit in moonlight on the rocks" (p. 47). At last that day arrived, and the little mermaid "went up through the surface of the water as light and clear as a bubble" (p. 50). Upon raising her head from her watery underworld, the little mermaid was besotted with images of untold beauty and amazement . . . a twinkly ship alive with a majestic display of fireworks in honor of the 16th birthday of the Prince, by whom the little mermaid was instantly besotted. The tranquil seas became "restless" and soon the great ship "had lay over on her side; and the water came rushing in" (p. 51). The sea soon became littered with shards of this great ship, and the little mermaid herself had to carefully move between the planks and large pieces of wood; "she herself had to look out for the beams and bits of wreckage that were drifting on the water" (p. 51) in order to make her way to the prince, whom she had seen slowly sink beneath the surface of the ocean. At last making her way to him, she "held his head above the water and let the waves carry her along with him" (p. 52). At last, they came in sight of land, so the little mermaid "swam with the handsome Prince to the beach . . . and laid him on the sand with his head carefully pillowed in the warm sunshine" (p. 52). As the bells of the nearby town sounded, a group of young girls approached the young prince, so the little mermaid swam out further into the sea to hide herself and watched what would happen to her poor prince. A young maiden approached the prince, and in her presence, he awakened "and smiled upon those who stood round him" (p. 52). But to the little mermaid, his true savior, "no smile came out to her, for of course, he didn't know that she had rescued him" (p. 52). The little mermaid was so saddened that she at once dove back beneath the waves and returned to her father's castle. Many an evening and morning passed and "it was her only comfort to fling her arm around her beautiful marble statue which was like the Prince" (p. 53). At last the little mermaid could bear her secret sorrow no longer, and confessed her heartbreak to one of her sisters, who carried the secret to two mermaids, who knew of the prince and his provenance. The little mermaid would swim much nearer to the shore; "here she would sit and gaze at the young Prince, who imagined he was quite alone in the clear moonlight" (p. 53). The little mermaid became "fonder and fonder of human beings and more and more she longed for their company" in a world that "seemed to her to be so much larger than her own" (p. 53). As her sisters were unable to answer her questions, she appealed to her grandmother who rightly called this realm "the lands above the sea" (p. 54). Her grandmother explained that while human beings' life term is "shorter" than mermaids that they have a "soul which can live forever" (p. 54). Mermaids can live much longer (300 years) but when "we cease to exist, we only become the foam on the surface of the water. We have not immortal souls, we shall never live again." "Why have not we an immortal soul?" asked the little mermaid mournfully; "I would give gladly all the hundreds of years that I have to live, to be a human being only for one day, and to have the hope of knowing the happiness of that glorious world above the stars" (p. 54).

"You must not think of that," said the old woman; "we feel ourselves to be much happier and much better off than human beings" (Andersen, 1837/1976, p. 54). "So I shall die," said the little mermaid, "and as the foam of the sea I shall be driven about never again to hear the music of the waves, or to see the pretty flowers nor the red sun. Is there anything I can do to win an immortal soul?" (p. 54).

> "No," said the old woman, "unless a man were to love you so much that you were more to him than his father or mother; and if all his thoughts and all his love were fixed upon you, and the priest placed his right hand in yours, and he promised to be true to you here and hereafter, then his soul would glide into your body you would obtain a share in the future happiness of mankind. He would give a soul to you and retain his own as well; but this can never happen. Your fish's tail, which amongst us is considered so beautiful, is thought on earth to be quite ugly; they do not know any better, and they think it necessary to have two stout props, which they call legs, in order to be handsome." (p. 54)

The little mermaid "couldn't forget the charming Prince and her sorrow at not possessing, like him, an immortal soul" (p. 55). Her sorrow and longing became so strong that the little mermaid decided to set off to see the sea witch, of whom she was very much afraid, for counsel. A treacherous journey she undertook, and she at last arrived at the grotto of the sea witch. Upon her arrival, the sea witch knew immediately why the little mermaid had arrived upon her doorstep:

> "I know well enough what you're after," said the sea witch. "How stupid of you! Still, you shall have your way, and it will bring you into misfortune, my lovely Princess. You want to get rid of your fish's tail, and in its place have a couple of stumps to walk on like a human being, so that the young Prince can fall in love with you, and you can win him and have an immortal soul." (p. 56)

Upon preparing a wicked potion for the little mermaid to drink, the sea witch explained what terrors would await the little mermaid:

> "Then your tail will divide in two and shrink up into what humans call 'pretty legs.' But it will hurt; it will be like a sharp sword going through you. Everyone who sees you will say that you are the loveliest human child they have ever seen. You will keep your graceful movements—no dancer can glide so lightly—but every step you take will feel as if you were treading upon a sharp knife, enough to make your feet bled. Are you ready to bear all that? If you are, I'll help you." (p. 56)

The evil sea witch then demanded her price for preparing such a draught: "this voice you will hand over to me; I demand the best that you have for the price of my draught" (p. 56). Then she cut off the mermaid's tongue, so that she became dumb, and would never again speak or sing.

The little mermaid made her way towards the surface of the sea, lay upon the shore, and drank the horrid tincture. She fell into a swoon from the painful incarnation, and when she awoke, she found standing before her the handsome young Prince.

> The Prince asked her who she was, and how she had come there, and she could only look back so gently and yet so sadly out of her deep-blue eyes; for of course she couldn't speak. Every step she took, as the witch had foretold, was as though she were treading on sharp knives and pricking gimlets; but she gladly put up with that. By the side of the Prince she went along as lightly as a bubble; and he and all of them marveled at the charm of her graceful movements. (Andersen, 1837/1976, p. 58)

Soon the little mermaid was regaled with the finest of silken robes. She attended a celebration in honor of the prince and his royal parents, and upon hearing the songs of the beautiful slaves, her heart sank, as she knew that "Oh, if only he knew that I gave my voice away for ever, in order to be with him" (p. 58). Soon there was dancing, and the little mermaid raised her lovely white arms, "lingered on the tips of her toes and then glided over the floor, dancing as no one had danced before . . . still she went on dancing, although every time her foot touched the ground it felt as though she were treading on sharp knives" (p. 59).

> Day by day she became dearer to the Prince. He loved her as one loves a dear, good child, but he didn't dream of making her his Queen, and yet she had to become his wife, or else she would never win an immortal soul, but on his wedding morning would be turned to foam on the sea. (p. 59)

But now the Prince was getting married they said—married to the pretty daughter of a neighboring King:

> At last she came . . . "A vision of perfect beauty"; "It's you!" cried the Prince. "You who rescued me, when I was laying half-dead on the shore." And he clasped his blushing bride in his arms. "Oh, I am too, too happy," said he to the little mermaid. "My dearest wish—more than I ever dared to hope for—has been granted me. My happiness will give you pleasure, because you're fonder of me than any of the others." (p. 61)

At this, the little mermaid's heart was broken, as she knew that his wedding morning would bring her death "and change her into foam on the sea" (p. 61).

> She knew this was the last evening she should ever see the Prince, for whom she had turned her back on kindred and home, given up her beautiful voice, and every day suffered hours of agony without his suspecting a thing. . . . She had no soul and could never win one. (p. 61)

As the night unfolded, and all fell into a silent slumber, the little mermaid alone was awake. She looked into the sea, and there her sisters appeared, their long beautiful hair now shorn:

> "We have given it to the witch, so that she might help us to save you from dying when to-night is over. She has given us a knife—look, here it is—do you see how sharp it is? Before sunrise, you must stab it into the Prince's heart. Then, when his warm blood splashes over your feet, they will grow together in a fish's tail, and you will become a mermaid once more; you will be able to come down to us in the water and live out your three hundred years before being changed into the dead salt foam of the sea. Make haste! Either he or you must die before the sun rises." (p. 62)

And then they sighed deeply and mournfully, and sank down beneath the waves.

The little mermaid "drew aside the purple curtain . . . and saw the lovely bride sleeping with her head resting on the Prince's breast" (Andersen, 1837/1976, p. 62).

> The knife quivered in the mermaid's hand—but then she flung it far out into the waves; they glimmered red where it fell, and what looked like drops of blood came oozing out of the water. With a last glance at the Prince from eyes half dimmed in death she hurled herself from the ship into the sea and felt her body dissolving into foam. (p. 62)

"'To whom am I coming?,' she asked, and her voice sounded like that of the other beings, more spiritual than any earthly music can record" (p. 62).

> "To the daughters of the air," answered the others. "A mermaid has no immortal soul and can never have one unless she wins the love of a mortal. Eternity, for her, depends on a power outside her. Neither have the daughters of the air an everlasting soul but by good deeds they can shape one for themselves. We shall fly to hot countries, where the stifling air of pestilence means death to mankind; we shall bring cool breezes. We shall scatter the fragrance of flowers through the air and send them comfort and healing. When for three hundred years we have striven to do the good we can, then we shall win an immortal soul and have share in mankind's eternal happiness." (p. 63)

"The little mermaid raised her crystal arms towards God's sun, and for the first time she knew the feeling of tears" (p. 63).

Cri de Coeur: **Undine and The Little Mermaid**

The stories of *Undine* (de la Motte Fouque, 1814/2002) and *The Little Mermaid* (Andersen, 1837/1976) are mythologems that reveal the development of consciousness in women who are estranged from personal, authentic feeling states and instead identify with the patrifocal collective. Like all mermaids, the very nature of Undine and the little mermaid is one of hybrid duality (like both Krishna and Hermes, notably)—creatures born of and under water, potent elemental chimerical entities required to endure a journey towards a new land, and a new consciousness. Like Psyche, these are journeys that require that the shadowy hinterlands and underworld be penetrated by an emerging consciousness. Indeed, each journey through such darkly vestiges leads to a new level of emerging consciousness and initiatory growth for Undine and the little mermaid. While there are many similarities shared between Undine and the little mermaid, there are also potent touchpoints of difference that serve to illuminate multi-dimensional aspects and developmental phases of an emerging feminine consciousness. I will discuss three such distinctions, each carrying pertinent archetypal information about the emergence and attributes of the feminine principle within these stories. The distinctions are as follows:

1. The transmission of feminine consciousness.
2. Feminine soul/lessness.
3. Death and its relationship to the chthonic feminine.

First, Undine has no native sisters, mother, or grandmother that can reflect her in her natural femininity, only a "mysterious Father . . . a powerful water-prince in the Mediterranean Sea [who] desired that his only daughter should become possessed of a soul, even though she must then endure many of the sufferings of those thus endowed" (p. 43). It becomes clear to us that it is Undine's *father's* wish for her (as his only daughter) that she become endowed with soul. While we know not whether Undine shared this longing, it also becomes clear that she accepts his longing for her as her *own*. Symbolically, this could be perceived as a surrender to her introjected animus in order to survive in the world. She accepts her father's desire for her, and completes *his* life mission through incarnating as a bride and thusly, a mortal woman. In other words, the element of the feminine which is missing in Undine's familial imprinting is replaced by a heightened relationship to her animus, to which she acculturated, and as such, it enabled her to function within the masculine psychic field of her family.

To be clear, Undine has an adoptive human mother, but not one that is grounded in the same chthonic and *elemental* feminine principle that Undine constellates. The little mermaid's mother has died, but she has five sisters and a (notably, *paternal*) grandmother that help to reflect her burgeoning feminine consciousness and formally prepare her for her odyssey, albeit through outer-world patternings of convention and tradition. (Interestingly, the little mermaid's grandmother is one of the few instances of dowager or crone-mermaid that I have encountered in this research. Ironically—and sadly—she displays overt animus-possession signatures rather than the ability to transmit true chthonic feminine wisdom to her granddaughters.) In each instance, the queen/mother is either dead or absent and the king/father rules the watery, underworld kingdom. This information tells us that these stories and characters are deeply ensconced within a patrifocal consciousness, and that of no choice of their own, both Undine and the little mermaid are daughters of their father:

> [A father's daughter] depreciates her own mother and identifies with her father. She is bright and ambitious and gets things done. . . . If she does not take time to discover her mother's strengths and reclaim her deep connection to the maternal bond, she may never heal her separation from the feminine. (Murdock, 1990, p. 34)

In the case of Undine and the little mermaid, the maternal and/or feminine was absent or, at the least, distanced through generational or adoptive circumstances: the subtext reveals that the feminine, through loss or displacement, was weakened, wounded, and at best, mediated through a patriarchal or animus-driven context (i.e., via the little mermaid's paternal grandmother).

> The return to the goddess for renewal in a feminine source-ground and spirit, is a vitally important aspect of a modern woman's quest for wholeness. . . . All too many modern women have not been nurtured by the mother in the first place. . . . They have grown up in the difficult home of abstract, collective authority. . . this inner connection is an initiation essential. . . .Without it we are not whole. [It requires] both a sacrifice of our identity as spiritual daughters of the patriarchy

> and a descent into the spiritual goddess, because so much of the power and passion of the feminine has been dormant in the underworld—in exile for five-thousand years. (Perera, 1981, p. 7)

The idea that the feminine incarnation of *mother* was too wounded or weakened to be authentically and affectively present in and for the lives of their young daughters is a metaphor that is very much alive within my personal mythology as well as within the greater collective:

> Our mothers were afflicted with a self-image of shame, degradation, self-doubt, and low self-esteem; our grandmothers were afflicted, too, back through how many generations? Most of us have no idea of the depth of the wounding of the feminine in the unconscious of both men and women. Our mothers and grandmothers were ravaged in the very cells of their bodies as we are ravaged. Few of them have had any way to access their unconscious shame. Jung argued that our actual parents are nominal. Our real parents are our ancestors. (Woodman, 1993, pp. 132-133)

When our mothers are unable to reflect our true feminine nature, we must look outside ourselves towards a masculine consciousness for soul.

The second most essential distinction between Undine and the little mermaid is one of incarnation and its relationship to soul. When we, as readers, are introduced to Undine, she is already articulated in human form. In fact, the readers are never clear if she has ever had a tail, although the narrative conveys that she, as did the little mermaid, had lived in a great crystal dome beneath the sea. Undine herself confessed her true identity to her husband on their wedding night as "a tender mermaid . . . an Undine" (de la Motte Fouque, 1814/2002, p. 42). In the story of the little mermaid, we are privy to her incarnation into embodied (albeit soulless) woman in the most painful of ways, sacrificing both voice and enduring physical agony with each human step she takes. "We learn early to be silent to the pain we feel. In the little mermaid's desire to have a soul, she sacrifices her voice and walks through life silent and in pain" (Burke, 2006, p. 21).

Within each story, in a trope that is congruent with classical mermaid mythology, each young mermaid maiden may only be ensouled upon matrimony and "closest union of affection" with a mortal man. Through her marriage to Knight Huldbrand, Undine was thusly endowed with soul:

> But all things aspire to be higher than they are. Thus, my father, who is a powerful water-prince in the Mediterranean Sea, desired that his only daughter should become possessed of a soul, even though she must then endure many of the sufferings of those thus endowed. Such as we are, however, can only obtain a soul by the closest union of affection with one of your human race. I am now possessed of a soul, and my soul thanks you, my inexpressibly beloved one, and it will ever thank you, if you do not make my whole life miserable. For what is to become of me, if you avoid and reject me? Still, I would not retain you by deceit. And if you mean to reject me, do so now, and return alone to the shore. I will dive into this brook, which is my uncle; and here in the forest, far removed from other friends, he passes his strange and solitary life. He is, however, powerful, and is esteemed and beloved by many great streams; and as he brought me hither to the fisherman, a light-hearted, laughing child, he will take me back again to my parents, a loving, suffering, and soul-endowed woman. (de la Motte Fouque, 1814/2002, p. 43)

While it is true that Undine's endowment with soul and initiation into a collective feminine consciousness via marriage did assuage her impulsive truancies and entrapments that she unconsciously and chthonically cathected, the fact remains that she is an earth-spirit, a child of the elements and that the chaotic vestiges of the natural world remain resonant. This reality—Undine as an agent of the natural and elemental world—creates an inescapable linkage between the realm of nature and its seeming divinely sanctioned lawlessness and the unconsciousness of at least *half* of this particular creature.

It is altogether different for the little mermaid. Despite the gravity of her sacrifice and adaptation towards a masculine consciousness, she does not become betrothed to her beloved prince. As she is mute (via surrendering her tongue), she is not able to express her feelings and her interior affective state. As a result, her beloved prince is unaware of her feelings for him, and he marries a beautiful princess from a nearby kingdom. Paradoxically, it is the little mermaid's sacrifice of feminine soul (in the form of authentic embodied feeling and expression) that cost her an initiatory encounter with love and marriage: a transpersonal soul. With each step the little mermaid took, it is "as if she were treading on knives" (Andersen, 1837/1976, p. 59), and yet, to her beloved prince (symbolic of her animus) she only smiled, and danced again quite readily, to please him, though each time "her foot touched the floor it felt as though she were treading on sharp knives" (p. 59).

Symbolically, this resonates for me. I too know this lost sense of feminine self. I too have offered to dance only more gracefully before the masculine gaze, all the while denying the agony of each hollow step. I too know the grief at having betrayed my feeling: I have spent far too much of my life unknowingly looking outside my self into the masculine prism for soul.

I am emerging.

Mermaids are beings of the hinterland; they flout the laws of the instinctual realms as well as that of an ensouled human consciousness. It is this very embodied duality and paradoxical dynamism that provides the link to recognizing that within the symbolic phenomenology of the mermaid exists the essential and primordial feminine instinct. Jungian analyst and author Monika Wikman captured this intersecting point of consciousness and the instinctual "erotic wilderness," through her illumination that

> the need to be in contact with mystery, unknowingness, and darkness is as crucial to the soul's life as any gains in consciousness. What are the gains in consciousness worth if we lose our rooting in the chaotic unknown, the erotic wilderness of the psyche that brings renewal of consciousness in the first place?

> Without experiential roots in the wilderness of the psyche, we lose connection with the original living spirit that is the healer, the uniter of opposites of which Jung and the alchemists spoke. (2004, p. xx)

Intriguingly, Wikman did not contextualize nor name this “mystery, unknowingness . . . darkness . . . chaotic unknown . . . erotic wilderness” as the feminine principle, but I very much recognize the presence of the soul qualities of the feminine within this passage.

The third sphere of distinction between Undine and the little mermaid is in their highly differentiated encounters with death. In the instance of the little mermaid, she is provided with the opportunity to spare her own life by taking that of her beloved. Her sisters emerge from the depths of the sea, with their long hair shorn as payment to the witch for this brief visit:

> “Before sunrise, you must stab it into the Prince’s heart. Then, when his warm blood splashes over your feet, they will grow together in a fish’s tail, and you will become a mermaid once more; you will be able to come down to us in the water and live out your three hundred years before being changed into the dead salt foam of the sea. Make haste! Either he or you must die before the sun rises.” (Andersen, 1837/1976, p. 62)

The little mermaid hovers above the sleeping body of her beloved prince, his bride resting upon his breast.

> The knife quivered in the mermaid’s hand—but then she flung it far out into the waves; they glimmered red where it fell, and what looked like drops of blood came oozing out of the water. With a last glance at the Prince from eyes half dimmed in death she hurled herself from the ship into the sea and felt her body dissolving into foam. (p. 62)

The little mermaid “hurled herself from the ship into the sea” and knew not where she was. In this gesture, we see a paradoxical incarnation of consciousness. On one pole, she embodies a certain conscientiousness; she is not able to kill her beloved. However, as her actions reflect, she once again would rather sacrifice her self in order to spare the life of the prince. Symbolically, this can be construed as a sacrifice of the psychic life of the feminine in order to spare the established masculine order of things—and perhaps an intolerance for differentiation and feminine consciousness via the return to the sea, symbol of unconsciousness. There are vagaries within this narrative sequence that are potentially illuminating. Notably, the little mermaid was never initiated into matrimony—and therefore—soulfulness. Her actions, therefore, may be congruent with an order, a way of being, or consciousness that exists *outside* a purely human logos. It may be that the little mermaid's actions are reflective of a less developed feminine consciousness (i.e., a lack of *differentiation*), or it may perhaps be indicative of a certain virginal instinctive consciousness.

Undine's encounter with death resulted in a radically different outcome: that of the murder of her beloved husband. Undine carries with her two "rules" from her watery precincts that govern her marriage to her Knight Huldbrand: that he never speak poorly of her or to her when they are near water, and that he always remain faithful to her during the duration of their marriage. As the story reveals, both of these vows are broken, and as such, Undine's Uncle Kuhleborn reminds her: "And yet, niece, you are subject to the laws of our element. . . . You are in duty bound to take away his life" (de la Motte Fouque, 1814/2002, p. 80). Undine remains compliant with the "laws" of her element, and as such,

> trembling with love and with the approach of death, she kissed him with a holy kiss; but not relaxing her hold she pressed him fervently to her, and as if she would weep away her soul. Tears rushed into the knight's eyes, and seemed to surge through his heaving breast, till at length his breathing ceases, and he fell softly back from the beautiful arms of Undine, upon the pillows of his couch—a corpse. (p. 80)

This is a very different sort of consciousness than the one enacted by the little mermaid. Despite her profound sorrow, Undine honored the "laws of [her] element" by obeying the command of her Uncle. This can be interpreted in at least two ways. It may be that Undine makes the conscious choice to honor the laws of the way of her oceanic underworld "element"—which despite its external patriarchal overtones, remains latently congruent with the realm of the unconscious and the feminine. In other words, perhaps Undine was acting congruently with the instinctive aspects of her elemental and chthonic nature. "When the heroine functions in accordance with the instinctive requirements of the psyche, she is the pattern of the conscious *feminine personality* [emphasis added]" (von Franz, 1993, p. 22).

In light of this possibility, Undine's compliance with the instinctual aspects of her feminine nature is a form of initiation towards a greater feminine consciousness. Paradoxically, this was not able to occur during Undine's embodiment as a mortal woman, but needed to be encountered once she had "regressed" towards a more authentic elemental and feminine psychic life. She needed to return to her natural plane (as elemental) in order to constellate a more articulated feminine consciousness. Metaphorically, this may illustrate that for the feminine principle, there is a paradoxical congruency between consciousness and the instinctual plane, and that what once may have been viewed as disparate and oppositional, are indeed part of a vibrant whole. In other words, perhaps it is that the more the feminine principle can make contact with an instinctual dimension, the more readily one is able to be initiated into a greater consciousness. (This, of course, has metaphorical relevance to the actual symbol of the mermaid as an entity not comprised of oppositional forces, but one that embodies a fluid psychic totality.)

Additionally, von Franz encapsulated the possibility that Undine simply acted *unconsciously* and congruently with "the dark aspect of the feminine nature goddess":

> According to mythological standards, there is also a feminine justice and a feminine principle of revenge. . . . A wrong attitude, not necessarily immoral but one not in accordance with nature is also avenged. . . . It could be called punishment by natural processes or revenge by the natural process of things. . . . Nature is sometimes harsh, severe, and cruelly revengeful. There is neither judgement nor rule, but the revenge of the dark aspect of the feminine nature goddess. (1993, pp. 38-39)

Intriguingly, this idea posits a rather antithetical premise to the preceding notion. This idea recognizes a chthonic and possibly cruel aspect to the feminine goddess, famously embodied within the Vedic goddess, Kali. In this light, it may be that Undine, despite her sorrow, simply acted in accordance with the instinctive patterning of her chthonic, unconscious nature. Von Franz further explicated that "if the woman is in Tao and functioning according to the inner laws of her being, she can afford that kind of feminine nastiness, and it is not animus possession" (p. 40). Strikingly, von Franz overtly spoke to the remaining third possibility within this triumvirate of possibilities. It simply may be that Undine is neither encountering an initiatory aspect yielding greater feminine consciousness, nor is she embodying and expressing her true chaotic dark essence as a "nature goddess"; it may be, perhaps, that Undine is simply obeying the dominant introjected patriarchal voice of her psyche. Despite a singular reference to her "parents," it is clear that Undine is a child with no authentic feminine reflection. She has been commanded into Being via the anima of her father and uncle. Her uncle was entirely clear about what was expected of her regarding "the laws of her element"—and if for a moment we, as readers, allow that her element is one of an entirely masculine matrix, than she certainly is not aware that there is choice available to her. She is commanded by the laws of the collective father, and as such, she submits. Of course, I cannot help leaning more hopefully into the depths and subtleties of complex feminine nature, one that understands and participates in the continuum between life and death, but I also cannot dismiss this notion of possible surrender to animus possession. To do so would be to deny the passages of my own fragile and yet consuming relationship to the masculine spheres. Perhaps it is so that Undine *feels* the loss of her husband but nonetheless recapitulates to the demands of the primitive and pervasive masculine by killing the conscious masculine? Ultimately, I cannot know for certain. I must allow the interstices of *not* knowing. Undine remains very alive for me; paradoxically, it is precisely her animal nature that I experience as so profoundly rehumanizing. In some ways, I feel that I have known her all my life and recognize her in ways that I have never known another. And yet, I carry within me a living uncertainty about her. She remains quixotic, shape-shifting, elusive, and intermittently tragic, potent, and lost.

I am afraid here of externalizing her; I want to feel her, to keep her alive.

> Let's leave it right there: images as instincts, perceived instinctually; the image, a subtle animal; the imagination, a great beast, a subtle body, with ourselves inseparably lodged in its belly: imagination, an animal mundi and an anima mundi, both diaphanous and passionate, unerring in its patterns and in all ways necessary, the necessary angel that makes brute necessity angelic; imagination, a moving heaven of theriomorphic gods in bestial constellations, stirring without external stimulation within our animal sense as it images its life in our world. (Hillman, 1991, p. 64)

Fairy Tail

And so I come to the sea in the dying light of the late afternoon. The soul can only tolerate so much bright light. I sit by the sea and listen; I trace my inhalations and exhalations with the rhythm of the waves. I place my bare legs before me, outstretching them, inner ankles kissing. I begin to wrap my legs in my pashmina scarf, binding them together. I feel them relax against this taught swaddle; there is nowhere for them to go.

"My fairy tail" I say aloud, not sure for a moment which version of the spelling Psyche intends. But I know. I am aware, as my legs are constrained, that so too are my breasts. This won't do. I slip my hand beneath my blouse and remove my bra, suddenly longing for my breasts to feel the golden warmth of the waning sun, the gentle cool mist of the sea. I imagine what this would feel like, the way the mermaid's breasts were bare and could feel the salty waters of the ocean and the perhaps cool air as she sunned herself upon a rock. I cannot be this free, here, now.

I put down my pen and close my eyes, suddenly aware that there is sadness, that there are tears. I feel lonely on this beach in the dying light of a descending sun. I close my eyes, place palms open and upwards upon my bound thighs, *my fairy tail,* and I listen.

Why do I feel so sad?

I think about Undine and the little mermaid. I think about how each mermaid needed to look outside of her self for a soul. I know deeply how this feels—this estrangement from authentic feeling. For so long, I did not know my own soul, so I sought to create it in the world around me. I thought if I worked harder, performed more, "did better," this little winged thing would come and dwell in me and I would feel "happy"—that my soul would come home. And I think how Undine had no mother, no grandmother (where *were* they?) to reflect who she is instead of seeing/sourcing herself through Father, through Uncle. This, too, I know. I do have a Mother—a beautiful one—but one that was so chronically psychically wounded by father, by brother, by husband, that she too did not dare to make contact with her deepest and most authentic feeling. A mother cannot inspire nor reflect that which she herself has not known. She had children to raise, and in the face of a brilliant but unstable ex-husband and father of her children, had stability to provide. So the water in her tears evaporated, and she became our "salt of the earth." There was no room for her mourning and scarlet sorrows (though we could nearly smell her grief).

And I think of the little mermaid, who so gladly sacrificed her tongue—let it be brutally cut out of her mouth—in order to marry a mortal man. How effortlessly she sacrificed her voice, it having been like sweet healing nectar to the world around her, in order to be loved by the masculine. And, too, how she gladly let her sinuous and lovely tail be split in two, torn asunder into human legs that with each graceful step she took, would greet her with the most agonizing physical pain. I know this . . . I remember this. I feel it now, my eyes welling with tears and a sudden longing to stop writing. Hasn't it been enough?

There is something to be named here, I know this for certain. Something arching for the light, to be known. My own loss, my own agonies, my own shame in giving away my voice, my body, in the name of hope, in the name of longing for soul. Shame is here, sorrow, too. And tears of grief for all that I have lost, all that my beautiful mother gave up. And her mother, too. How many generations does it go? And to what degree of separation before we arrive at women who were literally burned at the stake (the reality of this remains incomprehensible) for daring to touch more deeply into their own Feminine nature? Why do I feel like I remember this . . . that every cell in my body is screaming for me to remember? To know *this* fear, to know that my path has been cleared by the bravest, most beautiful women so I might have a chance at claiming my birthright—by being who I am meant to be.

I am cold. The sun is drawing closer to the sea, descending. Father Sun slipping silently into the watery underworld. The light of day giving way to the moon, to darkness, to the feminine: the death of a day. I listen now; the pulse of the waves has become louder as my vision becomes dimmed by the shadows of a sinking sun. I listen to the sound of my crying, the sound of the ocean, and know that this is the music of a soul, the song of my mermaids. I take off my shirt and let the dying light and dewy air envelop my naked breasts. I feel the cool air dry my inky, tear-stained cheeks, throat, breasts . . . and I remember.

Chapter IV
Conclusion

Summary of Previous Chapters

The writing of this thesis has been quite a circuitous journey. Chapter I introduced some of my personal connection to both the image and the stories of the mermaid. In many ways, I feel as though the mermaids have found me, that there are times that the spirits choose us to witness them (Wikman, 2004, p. 87). I brought forth a dream I had that was one of several unconscious, somatic encounters with the symbol of the mermaid that occurred throughout the writing process.

In Chapter II, I delved more deeply into the literary, historical, and mythopoeic aspects of the image of the mermaid, bringing forward the more ontological as well as mythological lineage of this ancient image. As there is little documentation within the canon of depth psychology about the image, it was necessary to work through the lens of archetypal psychology with authors and analysts such as Hillman and Eliade. Woodman and von Franz supported a more crystalline engagement with the feminine principle that very much came alive within Chapter III.

Chapter III, entitled "The Descent," was very much an organic and intimate encounter with the meaning of this image—a dropping down and away from the more cerebral and conscious activities that the Literature Review required. At the risk of sounding trite, Chapter III required a personal certain willingness to surrender, an engagement with the idiom that "if I leap, the net will appear." It was a process of learning to trust both the process and the emerging but vulnerable voice of the anima. The feeling quality of "The Descent" was both a sweetness and a sorrow; an image that comes to mind is that of a chrysalis. "Trusting the process forces us to let go of what we had been clinging to in order to find the matrix that truly holds us. This matrix is the feminine; trusting it opens doors we never have imagined. We are held by something greater than illusions" (Burke, 2006, p. 173).

Ideas for Further Research

So much came alive for me when writing this thesis, and it was difficult to put aside content that I sensed was yearning for a voice. The mermaid is a profoundly rich symbol, and one that leans deeply into alchemical principles. The idea of the uroboric qualities of the mermaid—specifically within her bicaudal tail, was rather difficult to resist researching more deeply. The mysteries of the *coincidentia oppositorum* remain very fascinating to me, and would likely be a rich vein of research and discourse. I was rather moved by the way that there is a transglobal and timeless saturation of mermaid mythology; a comparative analysis of the cultural meaning of the symbol of the mermaid feels equally as vibrant as a forum for further thought. The fact that mermaids (*with* exception) do not hail from a matrilineal family is also a quality I find curious and meaningful. Mermaids, too, very rarely give birth. The notion of mermaid as strictly a feminine presence without a realized maternal aspect is intriguing. Jungian analyst and author Nancy Qualls-Corbett spoke to the idea of a static versus active feminine principle, and its relationship to the maternal instinct, in very illuminating ways: "The active, dynamic aspect of feminine nature, that which promotes change and transformation, counterbalances the static, elemental aspect, the maternal, which although it provides for growth, is essentially conservative and protective" (1988, p. 65). The relationship between mermaids and Aphrodite, specifically, as well as other goddesses, is very much alive and to my mind, is a very intriguing lineage of thought and research.

The Tail End

> A god can do it. But tell me how
> a man can follow him through the narrow
> lyre. The human self is split; where two
> heartways cross, there is no temple for Apollo.
>
> Rilke, 1923/1987, p. 7

The image of the mermaid has felt like something of an electrification; she was wholly unsummoned, an emissary from the chthonic darkness, and arrived in my life with potent psychic voltage. As I found my way towards her, it is as though my blood stirred with a distinct remembrance. These deeper psychic activities of my unconscious came to life through the initiatory encounter of writing this thesis, and in many ways, were heralded by the chimerical presence of the mermaid.

At times, while writing this thesis, it has felt like I have been carrying water in a leaky vessel . . . small steps forward towards a greater understanding, and yet there have been persistent, regressive re-enactments of animus possession. I have had to accept the consequences of a life that is being turned inside out and be willing to traverse these new shadowy corridors; by all accounts, my old *logos*-infused map has proved useless in this new sovereign. I am aware of the ways in which I am newly coming to terms with a patriarchal consciousness with which I have been so unconsciously identified, and on a more personal level, the consequences I bear from finding little reflection outside my own father's anima. I remain amazed that I set forth on a journey to write about mermaids, and yet find myself confronting the Apollonic shadow of the father in the hinterlands of the haunted forests. There is a sorrow in this for me, and I am aware of a heart that at times, while stoking the alchemical fires of this thesis, has been overwhelmed by loss, grief, and at times, rage.

What is it that I do not want to say or cannot say? What is it that I am afraid to know, to make contact with? These questions are still alive for me—and perhaps always will be. Certainly, I am on more familiar terms with these questions and sense whispered responses that I recognize as my truth, but I also know that, like the morphology of the mermaid, the deepest wisdom may remain hidden beneath the surface. I think about this journey, this process of writing my thesis . . . the hundreds of hours I have spent achingly alone with only books and the artificial luminosity of my computer screen. I have learned that loneliness has different frequencies and hungers, and at times, it is the loneliness *itself* that has led to insight and illumination, and it may be that only in its clutches can the ego truly establish a creative relationship with the inner world and release its own destiny (Woodman, 1985, p. 42).

Like Undine and the little mermaid, I spent much of my life looking outside myself for soul. I discounted and sacrificed feeling aspects in order to survive: there was no inherent trusting of inner state. Sadly, I did not know there was another way. Faced with no other interior compass, my unconscious looked to my animus to survive in the world.

> An increasing number of women whose psychic center has always radiated around the father, real or imagined, are determined to go through the initiation. These women are by inner necessity creators in the Keatsian sense of "soul-makers," that is their quest for meaning drives them to find their own inner story. (Woodman, 1980, p. 33)

The "result" of this encounter, this walking across the hot embers of "quest for meaning," is a re-orientation of relationship to anima *and* animus, and consequently, relationship to self. Slowly, through making contact with story (my story *and* "her" story), through the watery descent into the unconscious matrix of image, through the cellular memory of scale, sinew, and tail, through the conscious rehabilitation of authentic but forsaken feeling, I invited Psyche to speak to—and through—me. Through this descent, the feminine principle slowly revealed itself to me, so that at last when I wearily arrived "where two heartways cross, *there is no temple to Apollo*" [emphasis added] (Rilke, 1923/1987, p. 7). There was no choice; I could *only enter* more deeply into the chthonic pulse of the feminine. "The feminine principle is 'that which makes something real,' the mystery which bestows reality upon the spirit. It dominates in all times when the spirit has died in its old form and needs rebirth" (von Franz, 2006, p. 132).

The mermaids have served as a mythological compass, guiding the way along this moonlit footpath, guiding me towards the instinctive healing function of the anima. It is the image of the anima that embodies the profound spiritual essence of human nature and ultimately, leads one to the Self (Qualls-Corbett, 1988). For me, it was necessary to establish a grounded and conscious relationship with the archetype of the Feminine before I could embrace the animus with vulnerability and courage (Singer, 1994). Being in conscious healing relationship with the anima is a portal to being in a conscious, rehabilitative relationship with the animus. It is the anima, specifically, that functions as the gateway, par excellence, to the integrative function of what Jung would call a *hieros gamos*—"the inner union of opposites whereby splits are healed" (Wikman, 2004, p. 19). I am deeply grateful to that chthonic aspect of Self that obeyed this command of the inner word and inner world, even when ignited with fear.

> She no longer scares me. Like most women, this woman of the depths is only frightening when her energy is shackled, contained, and denied expression. When she can move more freely, all the creatures of earth and sea come to her. We are refreshed and renewed in her presence. Women, and men too, have to remember how to find her. (Murdock, 1990, p. 94)

I recognize that the more grounded I am in the consciousness of my essential being, the more I can love the contrasexual and less organic aspect of Self: the animus and its outer world masculine embodiment. My relationship to the anima has been strengthened by the process of attending to the archaic whispers of the image of the mermaid, in the dark and too, the light.

> The shift from anima-mess to anima-vessel shows in various ways: as a shift from weakness and suffering to humility and sensitivity; from bitterness and complaint to a taste for salt and blood, from focus upon the emotional pain of a wound—its causes, perimeters, cures, to its imaginal depths. (Hillman, 1991, p. 161)

Healing the Split

As I drew closer to this image, I was immediately aware of its paradoxical qualities—the way the mermaid embodied multiple opposing forces: chthonic versus civilized, consciousness versus unconsciousness, upper versus lower, nature versus spirit. However, the more time I spent in her waters, the more I began to sense that rather than constellating a dichotomy of opposing forces, the image of the mermaid is a psychic totality. In other words, the mermaids have taught me that our natures *are* indeed cleaved, *and* that just as it remains mysterious where the animal and woman aspects of the mermaid begin and end, that this chasm is built into the very foundation of Self. It is her conflictual nature that leads the way towards psychic wholeness. It is so with each of us that there is an archaic aspect of "being at odds" with ourselves; our tail, though no longer appended to our physical form, very much remains alive psychically.

Integrating the tail, the inferior, the shadow aspects of self and life cast into the

> shadows by the adaptations and biases of consciousness—integrating the tail which one drags behind as one plows on ahead in life—this requires a careful consideration of where our shadow falls in all arenas of life. We then need to turn our attention toward it lovingly to incorporate those inferiorities into the flow of our life force as it finds new balance and integration. (Wikman, 2004, p. 270)

The work of analysis, both as analysand as well as analyst, is to learn to attend to this remembrance and recognition of our *human* tail, lovingly and courageously. Within psychological and intrapsychic principles, transformation occurs at the juncture, the intersection of consciousness and unconsciousness: the intrapsychic lacunae where flesh meets scales. Perhaps it is so that we must each learn to keep our tail *and* grow legs.

> Read me the bit
> again about the thing
> that is pure. . . .
> read that bit, the thing
> we cannot turn our eyes to,
> you begin it.
>
> Holloway, 1975, "Cone," as cited in Carson, 1998, p. 151

References

Andersen, H. C. (1976). *Eighty fairy tales* (R. P. Keigwinn, Trans.). New York, NY: Pantheon Books. (Original work published 1837)

Burke, S. (2006). *Up from the sea: A Jungian interpretation of "The little mermaid."* Unpublished master's thesis, Pacifica Graduate Institute, Carpinteria, CA.

Campbell, J. with Moyers, B. (1988). *The power of myth* (B. S. Flowers, Ed.). New York, NY: Bantam Doubleday.

Carson, A. (1998). *Eros the bittersweet.* Champaign, IL and London, England: Dalkey Archive Press.

Clark, K. (1984). *The nude: A study in ideal form*. Princeton, NJ: Princeton University Press.

de la Motte Fouque, F. (2002). *Undine* (F. E. Bunnett, Trans.). San Bernadino, CA: Borgo Press. (Original work published 1814)

Dinnerstein, D. (1999). *The mermaid and the minotaur: Sexual arrangements and human malaise.* New York, NY: Harper & Row.

Downing, C. (2007). *The goddess: Mythological images of the feminine*. Lincoln, NE: Authors Choice Press.

Edinger, E. F. (1995). *Mysterium lectures: A journey through C. G. Jung's Mysterium Coniunctionis*. Toronto, Canada: Inner City Books.

Eliade, M. (1976). *Myths, rites, symbols: A Mircea Eliade reader, vol. 2* (W. C. Beane & W. G. Doty, Eds.). New York, NY: Harper Colophon.

Eliade, M. (1991). *Images and symbols: Studies in religious symbols* (P. Mairet, Trans.). Princeton, NJ: Princeton University Press. (Original work published 1952)

Eliot, T. S. (2001). *The waste land and other writings*. New York, NY: Modern Library.

Emerson, R. W. (1910). *Journals of Ralph Waldo Emerson with annotations* (E. W. Emerson & W. E. Emerson, Eds.). Boston, MA: Houghton Mifflin.

Estés, C. P. (1992). *Women who run with the wolves: Myths and stories of the wild woman archetype.* New York, NY: Ballantine Books.

Felty, D. W. (2002). The spirit of water. Retrieved from http://northstargallery.com/mermaids/MermaidHistory2.htm

Franz, M.-L., von. (1980). *The psychological meaning of redemption motifs in fairytales.* Toronto, Canada: Inner City Books.

Franz, M.-L. von. (1992). *The golden ass of Apuleius.* Boston, MA: Shambhala.

Franz, M.-L. von. (1993). *The feminine in fairy tales.* Boston, MA: Shambhala.

Franz, M.-L. von. (1996). *The interpretation of fairy tales* (Rev. ed.). Boston, MA: Shambhala.

Franz, M.-L., von. (2006). Psychological commentary. In M. Ibn Umail, *Corpus alchemicum arabicum: Book of the explanations of the symbols Kitab Halll ar-Rumuz* (Psychological commentary by M.-L. von Franz) (T. Abt & W. Madelung, Eds.). Zurich, Switzerland: Living Human Heritage.

Goodchild, V., & Romanyshyn, R. (2003). *Doing research with soul in mind.* Carpinteria, CA: Authors.

Graham, J. (2007). Prologue. In M. Lao, *Seduction and the secret power of women: The lure of sirens and mermaids* (John Oliphant of Rossie, Trans.) (pp. ix-x). Rochester, VT: Park Street Press. (Original work published 1998)

Harding, M. E. (1971). *Woman's mysteries: Ancient and modern.* Boston, MA: Shambhala.

Heaney, S. (1981). *Preoccupations: Selected prose, 1968-1978.* New York, NY: Farrar, Straus and Giroux.

Hillman, J. (1972). *The myth of analysis: Three essays in archetypal psychology.* Evanston, IL: Northwestern University Press.

Hillman, J. (1975). *Re-visioning psychology.* New York, NY: Harper Collins.

Hillman, J. (1991). *A blue fire: Selected writings by James Hillman* (T. Moore, Ed.). New York, NY: Harper Collins.

Hollis, J. (2000). *The archetypal imagination.* College Station, TX: Texas A & M University Press.

Humbert, E. (1988). *C. G. Jung: The fundamentals of theory and practice* (R. G. Jalbert, Trans.). Wilmette, IL: Chiron. (Original work published 1984)

Hyde, L. (1998). *Trickster makes this world: Mischief, myth, and art.* New York, NY: Farrar, Straus, and Giroux.

Jordan, N. (Writer/Director). (2010). *Ondine* [Motion picture]. Ireland/USA: Wayfare Entertainment.

Jung, C. G. (1968). Individual dream symbolism in relation to alchemy. In H. Read, M. Fordham, G. Adler, and W. McGuire (Eds.), *The collected works of C. G. Jung.* (R. F. C. Hull, Trans.) (Vol. 12, pp. 39-224). Princeton, NJ: Princeton University Press. (Original work published 1936)

Jung, C. G. (1969). A psychological approach to dogma of the trinity. In H. Read, M. Fordham, G. Adler, & W. McGuire (Eds.), *The collected works of C. G. Jung* (R. F. C. Hull Trans.) (2nd ed., Vol. 11, pp. 148-200). Princeton, NJ: Princeton University Press. (Original work published 1948)

Jung, C. G. (1969a). Archetypes of the collective unconscious. In H. Read, M. Fordham, G. Adler, and W. McGuire (Eds.), *The collected works of C. G. Jung.* (R. F. C. Hull, Trans.) (Vol. 9i, pp. 3-41). Princeton: Princeton University Press. (Original work published 1954)

Jung, C. G. (1969b). On the psychology of the trickster-figure. In H. Read, M. Fordham, G. Adler, and W. McGuire (Eds.), *The collected works of C. G. Jung.* (R. F. C. Hull, Trans.) (Vol. 9i, pp. 255-272). Princeton: Princeton University Press. (Original work published 1954)

Jung, C. G. (1969). The transcendent function. In H. Read, M. Fordham, G. Adler, & W. McGuire (Eds.), *The collected works of C. G. Jung* (R. F. C. Hull, Trans.) (Vol. 8, pp. 67-91). Princeton, NJ: Princeton University Press. (Original work published 1957)

Jung, C. G. (1971). Definitions. In H. Read, M. Fordham, G. Adler, & W. McGuire (Eds.) (H. G. Baynes, Trans., rev. R. F. C. Hull), *The collected works of C. G. Jung* (Rev. ed., Vol. 6, pp. 408-486). Princeton, NJ: Princeton University Press. (Original work published 1921)

Jung, C. G. (1977). The development of personality. In H. Read, M. Fordham, G. Adler, and W. McGuire (Eds.), *The collected works of C. G. Jung* (R. F. C. Hull, Trans.) (2nd ed., Vol. 17, pp. 167-186). Princeton, NJ: Princeton University Press. (Original work published 1954)

Jung, C. G. (1989). *Memories, dreams, reflections* (A. Jaffé, Ed.) (R. Winston & C. Winston, Trans.) (Rev. ed.). New York: Vintage Books. (Original work published 1961)

Kalsched, D. (1996). *The inner world of trauma: Archetypal defenses of the personal spirit*. New York, NY: Routledge.

Lao, M. (2007). *Seduction and the secret power of women: The lure of sirens and mermaids* (John Oliphant of Rossie, Trans.). Rochester, VT: Park Street Press. (Original work published 1998)

Lum, P. (1951). *Fabulous beasts*. London: Thames and Hudson.

MacDonald, G. (2010). *The fantastic imagination.* Retrieved from http://www.george-macdonald.com/etexts/nonfiction/fantastic_imagination.html

Mann, A. T., & Lyle, J. (1995). *Sacred sexuality.* London: Vega.

Meade, M. (2006). *The water of life: Initiation and the tempering of the soul.* Seattle, WA: Greenfire Press.

Melusine. (2010). In *Symbol dictionary*. Retrieved from http://symboldictionary.net?p=1153

Murdock, M. (1990). *The heroine's journey: Woman's quest for wholeness*. Boston, MA: Shambhala.

Musker, J., & Ashman, H. (Producers), & Clements, R., & Musker, J. (Directors) (1989). *The little mermaid* [Motion picture]. USA: Walt Disney Pictures.

Nietzsche, F. (1966). *Beyond good and evil: Prelude to a philosophy of the future* (W. Kaufmann, Trans.). New York, NY: Vintage Books. (Original work published 1886)

Perera, S. B. (1981). *Descent to the goddess: A way of initiation for women*. Toronto, Canada: Inner City Books.

Phillpotts, B. (1980). *Mermaids*. New York, NY: Ballantine Books.

Qualls-Corbett, N. (1988). *The sacred prostitute: Eternal aspects of the feminine.* Toronto, Canada: Inner City Books.

Rilke, R. M. (1987). *Sonnets to Orpheus* (D. Young, Trans). Middleton, CT: Wesleyan University Press. (Original work published 1923)

Romanyshyn, R. D. (2007). *The wounded researcher: Research with soul in mind.* New Orleans, LA: Spring Journal Books.

Singer, J. (1994). *Boundaries of the soul: The practice of Jung's psychology*. New York, NY: Anchor.

Tseëlon, E. (1995). *The little mermaid*: An icon of women's condition in patriarchy, and the human condition of castration. *International Journal of Psychoanalysis*, 76, 1017-1030.

Ulanov, A., & Ulanov, B. (2004). *Transforming sexuality: The archetypal world of anima and animus*. Boston, MA: Shambhala.

Watkins, M. (1984). *Waking dreams*. Woodstock, CT: Spring Publications.

Wikman, M. (2004). *Pregnant darkness: Alchemy and the rebirth of consciousness.* Berwick, ME: Nicolas-Hays.

Woodman, M. (1980). *The pregnant virgin: A process of psychological transformation.* Toronto, Canada: Inner City Books.

Woodman, M. (1992). Introduction. In M. Woodman with K. Danson, M. Hamilton, & R. G. Allen, *Leaving my father's house: A journey to conscious femininity* (pp. 1-7). Boston, MA: Shambhala.

Woodman, M. (1993). *Conscious femininity: Interviews with Marion Woodman.* Toronto, Canada: Inner City Books.

CPSIA information can be obtained
at www.ICGtesting.com
Printed in the USA
LVIW010716061112
306042LV00005B